BRANDEIS
AND AMERICA

BRANDEIS AND AMERICA

Edited by
NELSON L. DAWSON

THE UNIVERSITY PRESS OF KENTUCKY

Frontispiece: Louis D. Brandeis, ca. 1931.
Courtesy of the University of Louisville
School of Law.

Copyright © 1989 by The University Press of Kentucky

Scholarly publisher for the Commonwealth,
serving Bellarmine College, Berea College, Centre
College of Kentucky, Eastern Kentucky University,
The Filson Club, Georgetown College, Kentucky
Historical Society, Kentucky State University,
Morehead State University, Murray State University,
Northern Kentucky University, Transylvania University,
University of Kentucky, University of Louisville,
and Western Kentucky University.

Editorial and Sales Offices: Lexington, Kentucky 40506-0336

Library of Congress Cataloging-in-Publication Data

Brandeis and America / Nelson L. Dawson, editor.
  p. cm.
Bibliography: p.
Includes index.
ISBN 0-8131-1690-2 :
  1. Brandeis, Louis Dembitz, 1856-1941. 2. Judges—United States
—Biography. I. Dawson, Nelson L.
KF8745.B67A45 1989
347.73'14—dc 19
[347.30714]   89-30929

Contents

Introduction   1
NELSON L. DAWSON

Chronology   5
JANET B. HODGSON

The Propriety of Brandeis's Extrajudicial Conduct   11
DAVID J. DANELSKI

Brandeis and the New Deal   38
NELSON L. DAWSON

Brandeis, Judaism, and Zionism   65
ALLON GAL

Brandeis and the Progressive Movement   99
DAVID W. LEVY

Brandeis and the Living Constitution   118
PHILIPPA STRUM

The Brandeis Agenda   133
MELVIN I. UROFSKY

Suggested Reading   153
JANET B. HODGSON

Contributors   155

Index   157

BRANDEIS
AND AMERICA

Introduction

NELSON L. DAWSON

Louis D. Brandeis is a figure of perennial significance. Brilliant lawyer, innovative reformer, seminal thinker, and judicial giant, Brandeis merits all the scholarly attention he received during his lifetime and in the years since his death in 1941. Historiography does not always follow a predictable pattern. Subjects long neglected suddenly come into vogue while popular topics are strangely ignored. But whatever the causes of historiographical fluctuation—and they are undoubtedly complex—it is clear that Brandeis has always attracted considerable academic attention and that we are in a particularly productive phase of Brandeis scholarship.

The first era in Brandeis studies culminated in the publication of Alpheus T. Mason's 1946 biography *Brandeis: A Free Man's Life*. Mason's judicious work was based largely on the sources available during Brandeis's lifetime; some were balanced and some were uncritically laudatory. Mason's book, valuable as it has been, suffers from some of the defects characteristic of biographies written close to the life spans of their subjects. It is not surprising that the book becomes weaker during the description of the latter part of Brandeis's career. Mason's coverage of the New Deal years is cursory, and there is also an inevitable lack of historical perspective. However, none of these defects detract from the work's valuable pioneering contribution.

The period from 1946 to 1971 is a transitional era in Brandeis scholarship, characterized most notably perhaps by a number of memoirs of Brandeis by former law clerks, other close associates, and various New Deal figures. Most of these works are positive, but some, particularly by New Deal rivals such as Rexford Tugwell, are unfavorable.

The third stage of Brandeis scholarship began in 1971 with the publication of his letters, which are being edited by David W. Levy and Melvin I. Urofsky; two additional volumes are forthcoming. The year 1971 was also the year Urofsky's seminal survey of Brandeis's thought, *A Mind of One Piece: Brandeis and American Reform*, was published. These works and the availability of new manuscript sources have contributed to a steady increase in the number of new books, including several full-length biographies, as well as to a burgeoning periodical literature.

This latest phase of Brandeis scholarship has not only resulted in a steady expansion of knowledge about Brandeis and his career but also generated productive debate over several key issues relating to his significance.

There is the mystery of Brandeis's personality. While it would clearly be an exaggeration to describe him as Winston Churchill once described the Soviet Union—"a riddle wrapped in a mystery"—it is true that there remains much to be learned about his inner life. The more recent biographies by Leonard Baker, Lewis J. Paper, and Philippa Strum have helped to dispel some of the mystery, but they have not eliminated it altogether.

Brandeis's economic views—best characterized by his lifelong opposition to "bigness"—have been criticized by earlier conservatives who denounced them as evidence of his hostility to corporate America and by New Deal liberals who dismissed them as evidence of a nostalgic Jeffersonianism locked in Quixotic combat with the exigencies of twentieth-century business evolution. More recent scholars, notably Thomas K. McCraw, have moved beyond these earlier categories to subject Brandeis's economic philosophy to a searching analysis by calling into question the adequacy of his grasp of the varieties of corporate structure and their implications for economic policy. The debate on Brandeis's economic philosophy continues.

Perhaps the most significant of the current issues in Brandeis scholarship—and certainly the one that has received the greatest attention—is the question of judicial propriety. The remarkable range of Brandeis's political activities before his 1916 Supreme Court appointment has long been understood. The extent of his extrajudicial activities after 1916, however, has received less attention. Brandeis's contemporaries, both associates and rivals, knew of at least some of his activities, and later scholars began supplying more details. The issue, which had never been wholly neglected, came into prominence in 1982 with the publication of Bruce A. Murphy's *The Brandeis/Frankfurter Connection: The Secret Political Activities of Two Supreme Court Justices*. The critical tone of the book, reinforced by the publisher's sensationalistic marketing efforts, ensured that it would stimulate a reevaluation of Brandeis's extrajudicial activities, particularly during the New Deal, as well as an intense debate over the validity of Murphy's view of Brandeis and Frankfurter.

There are other aspects of Brandeis's career that are receiving renewed attention as well. His relationship to the Progressive movement is subject to continual study as historians seek to grapple with the bewildering variety of Brandeis's reform activities in the context of an ongoing debate over the nature of progressivism. Brandeis's relationship to Zionism is another intriguing subject that bears on the mystery of his personality, particularly the nature of his ethnic identity. In the light of all these issues clamoring for renewed attention, one is almost tempted to take his judicial accomplishments for granted, and yet this subject has by no means been exhausted.

This is clearly a dynamic period in Brandeis studies. The present collection of essays is particularly timely because it offers a fresh examination of the current issues. It is offered not only as a useful assessment of current scholarship but also in the hope that it will help stimulate further study. Even a superficial glance at the titles of the essays in this book reveals the range of Brandeis's interests—from general involvement in social and economic reform to intense concern with constitutional issues, Zionism, progressivism, and the New Deal. It is difficult to think of any major area of American life, with the exception of diplomacy, in which Brandeis was not deeply engaged. A profound consistency of social philosophy under-girded his varied activities; and yet if he had—in the memo-rable phrase used to describe this intellectual unity—a mind of one piece, he was also, as the diversity of these essays demonstrates, a man of many parts.

The essays in this book were originally presented as papers at the Brandeis Conference held in Louisville, Kentucky, on April 23-24, 1987. The conference, sponsored by the National Endowment for the Humanities, came from the efforts of the staff of the University of Louisville Archives. Dwayne Cox headed the grant application process and was assisted by Janet B. Hodgson and Cynthia Stevenson under the super-vision of university archivist William J. Morison. The Filson Club, headed by presidents Ronald R. Van Stockum and C. Hayden Edwards and director James R. Bentley, offered the collected papers to The University Press of Kentucky as a member of the Press consortium. Valuable support and coun-sel were also provided by the publications advisory committee of The Filson Club's board of directors, consisting of Philip P. Ardery, Kenneth Cherry, John S. Moremen, and John Ed Pearce.

Chronology

JANET B. HODGSON

1856 Nov. 13 Born, Louisville, Kentucky
1872 May Brandeis family leaves for three-year stay in Europe
1873 Sept. Enrolls in Annen-Realschule, Dresden, Germany
1875 May Returns to United States
Sept. Enrolls in Harvard Law School
1877 June Graduates Harvard Law School, first in class
Sept. Begins one year of graduate study at Harvard
1878 Sept. Begins law practice in St. Louis, Missouri, with James Taussig
1879 July Begins Boston law partnership with Samuel D. Warren
1882 Sept. Teaches course on evidence at Harvard Law School
1886 Sept. Organizes and becomes secretary of Harvard Law School Association
1889 Nov. Argues first case before United States Supreme Court
1890 Dec. Writes "Right to Privacy" article with Warren, published in *Harvard Law Review*
1891 March 23 Marries Alice Goldmark
1892 Fall Teaches courses on business law at Massachusetts Institute of Technology
1893 Feb. 27 First daughter, Susan, born
1896 April 25 Second daughter, Elizabeth, born
1897 Jan. 1 Law firm changes name to Brandeis, Dunbar, and Nutter

1900 March   Leads fight for preservation of municipal subway systems when Boston builds Washington Street subway

Summer   Joins Edward A. Filene and others in formation of Public Franchise League

1903 March   Helps organize the Good Government Association

1904 April 21   Addresses Boston Typothetae on industrial relations

1905 April 18   Retained as counsel to New England Policy-Holders' Committee

May 4   Addresses Harvard Ethical Society, "The Opportunity in the Law"

Oct. 26   Addresses Boston Commercial Club, "Life Insurance: The Abuses and the Remedies"

Nov. 28   Addresses New Century Club, "What Loyalty Demands"

1906 Nov. 26   Massachusetts Savings Bank Insurance League organized

1907 June 26   Massachusetts Savings Bank Life Insurance bill signed into law

Oct. 19   Refuses chance to run for mayor of Boston

Nov.   Publishes "How Boston Solved the Gas Problem," in *American Review of Reviews*

1908 Jan. 15   Argues *Muller* v. *Oregon* before the United States Supreme Court

Feb. 11   Addresses New England Dry Goods Association, Boston, "The New England Transportation Monopoly"

May 8   Presents an antimerger bill to the Massachusetts legislature

1909 June 19   Publishes "Boston and Maine Pensions," in *The Survey*

1910 Jan. 7   Retained by *Colliers* as counsel in Ballinger case

May 27-28   Summation in Ballinger case

July 21   Enters New York Garment Workers' strike as negotiator

Aug.   Agrees to become counsel for the Committee of

Commercial Organizations to oppose advanced freight rates

Sept. 2   Garment Workers' Protocol agreement signed

Dec.   Formation of National Progressive Republican League

1911 Jan. 17   Presents argument before Interstate Commerce Commission in the Advanced Freight Rate case

March 27   Addresses Economic Club of New York, "New Conception of Industrial Efficiency"

April 2   Addresses Boston Central Labor Union, "Organized Labor and Efficiency"

June 10   Publishes "The Road to Social Efficiency," in *The Outlook*

Sept.   Endorses Robert LaFollette, Sr., as presidential candidate

Nov. 28   Publishes "Using Other People's Money," in *New York American*

1912 June 19   Speaks at Brown University, "Business—A Profession"

July 10   Endorses Woodrow Wilson for president

Aug. 28   Conference with Woodrow Wilson at Sea Girt, New Jersey

Sept.   Begins campaign speaking tour for Wilson

Sept. 14   Publishes "Trusts, Efficiency, and the New Party," in *Colliers*

Sept. 21   Publishes "Trusts, the Export Trade, and the New Party," in *Colliers*

1913 April 7   Offered chairmanship of United States Commission on Industrial Relations by President Wilson

May 19   Declines chairmanship of Commission on Industrial Relations

July 18   Joins executive committee of Federation of American Zionists

Nov. 22   Publishes first article on "Breaking the Money Trust," in *Harper's*

1914 Aug. 30   Accepts chairmanship of Provisional Executive Committee on General Zionist Affairs

Dec. 16-17   Argues Oregon minimum wage case before Supreme Court

Books published, *Other People's Money* and *Business—A Profession*

1915 April 6 Gives talk on literacy test at New Century Club
April 25   Addresses Eastern Council of Reform Rabbis, "The Jewish Problem and How to Solve It"
July 5   Gives talk at Faneuil Hall, Boston, "True Americanism"

1916 Jan. 3   Addresses Chicago Bar Association, "The Living Law"
Jan. 24   Speaks at Carnegie Hall, New York, "Jewish Rights and the Congress"
Jan. 28   Nominated by Woodrow Wilson to the United States Supreme Court
June 1   United States Senate confirms nomination of Brandeis to Supreme Court
Aug. 10   Asked by Wilson to serve on Mexican arbitration commission; Brandeis declines

1917 April 23   Meets Arthur Balfour to discuss possible British mandate over Palestine

1918 May 25   Proposes reorganization of American Zionist movement

1919 June 14   Sails for England
July 8   Arrives in Palestine
Aug.   Attends Zionist meetings in London

1920 June 13   Sails for London and World Zionist conference
July 7   Addresses World Zionist conference, "The Upbuilding of Palestine"
Aug. 29   Addresses Executive Committee of Zionist Organization of America, "Review of the London Conference"

1921 April 26   Meets Albert Einstein
June 5-7   Attends Zionist convention in Cleveland, Ohio
June 19   Resigns honorary presidency of World Zionist Organization
Dec. 19   Dissents in Truax and American Lumber cases before the Court

1922 April   Daughter Susan opens law office in New York City

1924 Sept. 24   Begins donations of books and pamphlets to
the University of Louisville Library

1925 July 2   Daughter Elizabeth marries Paul Raushenbush
Oct. 25   Daughter Susan becomes first woman to argue
case before the Supreme Court
Dec. 30   Daughter Susan marries Jacob Gilbert

1926 Nov. 2   First grandchild, Louis Brandeis Gilbert, is born
Nov. 13   Celebrates his 70th birthday

1927 May 16   Dissents in Whitney case
Aug. 22   Turns down last-minute appeal in Sacco and
Vanzetti case

1928 May 28   Dissents in Quaker City Cab case
June 4   Dissents in Olmstead case
Aug. 8   Brother Alfred dies

1929 Nov. 29   Makes first public Zionist appearance since
1921

1930 July 1   Brandeis/Mack slate elected by Zionist Organization of America

1932 March 21   Dissents in New State Ice Company case

1934 June 7   Meets with President Roosevelt on unemployment compensation bill

1936 Nov. 13   Celebrates his 80th birthday

1939 Feb. 13   Resigns from the Supreme Court

1941 Oct. 1   Suffers heart attack
Oct. 5   Brandeis dies

1945 Oct. 12   Alice Goldmark Brandeis dies

The Propriety of Brandeis's Extrajudicial Conduct

DAVID J. DANELSKI

The first scholarly work to consider extensively Louis D. Brandeis's extrajudicial activity was Alpheus T. Mason's *Brandeis: A Free Man's Life*.[1] Published in 1946, it portrayed Brandeis as a modern hero—a "crusader," a "cloistered warrior," a "prophet," and a "stickler for proprieties."[2] It also portrayed him as an off-the-bench activist who drafted provisions for party platforms, advised President Wilson and members of his administration, provided leadership to the Zionist movement, suggested topics to journal editors for articles on policy matters, and influenced the policy views of those in power.[3] Mason never questioned the propriety of any of those activities, but he did provide explicit and tacit justifications for Brandeis's conduct.

Mason's discussion of Brandeis's advice in the appointment of William G. McAdoo as director general of railroads in 1917 illustrates explicit justification. In December of that year, Joseph P. Tumulty, the president's secretary, asked Interstate Commerce Commissioner Robert W. Wooley to seek Brandeis's support of McAdoo. According to Mason, Brandeis was sympathetic but "flatly refused to go to the White House in McAdoo's behalf."[4] Mason then reported:

> "What if the President were to ask you to come?" Tumulty inquired. "That would be a command, and I should obey," the Justice replied.
> It was then agreed that Tumulty would take up the

matter with the President and that Brandeis might expect an invitation from the President to call at the White House the following Sunday afternoon. At 4:45 P.M., Sunday, December 9, no word having come from the President, the Justice telephoned Wooley that he was at a loss as to what to do. Wooley promptly notified Tumulty, who said that he had discussed the matter with Wilson the day before, that his reaction to the suggested invitation had been favorable, and a memorandum had been placed on his desk.

"You see, Bob," Tumulty explained, "Woodrow Wilson is Scotch-Irish. When the Irish in him is on the job, he is wonderful. The Scotch seems to have the upper hand today."

At exactly 5 P.M. the President himself, accompanied by two Secret Service men, appeared unannounced at the Justice's apartment. "I could not request you to come to me," Wilson explained, "and I have therefore come to you to ask your advice."[5]

Mason concluded his report with this statement. "The President, like Brandeis, deemed it improper to ask a justice of the Supreme Court to the White House on a matter necessarily political. After a conference of about three-quarters of an hour, the President thanked Brandeis, told him he would appoint McAdoo, and left. Both men had exhibited a high conception of the proprieties of judicial office."[6]

Mason's discussion of Brandeis's participation in drafting a partisan political statement (called "The Document") illustrates tacit justification. In the early twenties, Brandeis kept in close touch with ex-President Wilson, who, broken politically and physically, had withdrawn to his home in Washington. At Wilson's request, Brandeis met with a group of loyal Wilson supporters for the purpose of formulating principles upon which the Democratic party might make a comeback in 1924. "By April 9, 1922," wrote Mason, "Wilson had assembled the group's several pieces into a single document nearly seven pages long. It was a ringing manifesto for an American conception of social justice. To Wilson it was 'satisfactory'—'a very clear and self-consistent document.' Republican leadership was bitterly denounced as the 'most partisan, prejudiced, and unpatriotic coterie that ever misled the Senate of the United States; . . . the country will never be restored to its merited prestige until their work is undone.' A clarion call went out to the Democratic party to return the country to prestige.'"[7] Mason suggested that Brandeis participated in the drafting of the partisan statement because of affection for Wilson. Moreover, Brandeis's responses to Wilson, wrote Mason, were "confidential" and "usually stated in general terms," and Brandeis counseled against using the statement in the election campaign of 1922.[8] "Ammunition so potent should not be dissipated," Brandeis told Wilson. "You have taught us the lesson of watchful waiting."[9]

Mason's portrayal of Brandeis as observing not only the normal strictures of judicial propriety but gratuitously enlarging them remained the conventional image of the justice for a quarter of a century. In 1971, however, Melvin I. Urofsky criticized Brandeis's participation in drafting "The Document" as improper. "The country would have been rightly upset," wrote Urofsky, "if it had discovered a Supreme Court Justice working to draft a party platform in order to get Democrats in power."[10]

Urofsky's charge of impropriety was mild compared to Bruce Allen Murphy's charges in 1982. The most serious of Murphy's charges were that Brandeis had threatened to hold legislation unconstitutional if his policy views were not followed by the Roosevelt administration and that Brandeis, while on the Supreme Court, had paid Felix Frankfurter a substantial annual stipend for political activities to further Brandeis's policy goals.[11] The *New York Times* regarded the latter charge important enough for front-page coverage and a critical editorial. "[T]he Brandeis-Frankfurter arrangement," stated the *Times*, "was wrong. It serves neither history nor ethics to judge it more kindly. . . . [T]he prolonged, meddlesome Brandeis-Frankfurter arrangement violates ethical standards."[12]

Since 1982, Lewis J. Paper, Philippa Strum, Leonard Baker, and David C. Gross published book-length biographies of

Brandeis.[13] Each dealt with one or more of the charges made by Urofsky and Murphy. As to Brandeis's participation in drafting "The Document," Paper wrote that "Brandeis certainly knew that most people would have frowned on his collaboration with Wilson on a political matter." But Paper thought that Brandeis's actions had been "discreet." There had been "no speeches, no press releases, just some correspondence and some private meetings, most of them at Wilson's house on S Street in northwest Washington."[14] Paper discussed the Brandeis-Frankfurter financial arrangement in more detail. He acknowledged that in the post-Watergate era, there was merit to the view that the arrangement would give the appearance of impropriety. "But," he added, "Brandeis and Frankfurter lived in a different time. For them, the financial support did not reflect an employer-employee relationship. More than anything, it symbolized the close emotional and intellectual bond between the two men."[15] After further discussion of Murphy's charge, Paper concluded that the Brandeis-Frankfurter financial arrangement was not improper.

Strum was more critical of Brandeis's participation in the drafting of "The Document." She thought the correspondence between Brandeis and Wilson on the matter was important because of the light "it sheds on the difficulty Brandeis had containing himself within the traditional boundaries of judicial ethics."[16] Overall, Strum was more troubled by Brandeis's extrajudicial activities than any of Brandeis's recent biographers. Near the end of her book, she concluded ambivalently: "Brandeis seems to have been both unethical and honest: he immersed himself in the formulation of policy in a most unjudicial manner, but he judged the cases that came before him according to the legal principles he enunciated publicly."[17]

Baker thought that Brandeis's participation in the drafting of "The Document" was "one of his few judicial 'indiscretions.' "[18] Like Mason, Baker said that Brandeis had acted in the matter out of affection for Wilson. Baker defended Brandeis's financial arrangement with Frankfurter as well as his other extrajudicial activities. "[T]here were no rules to define whether Brandeis's extrajudicial activities were improper," wrote Baker, "only traditions which he did not push beyond accepted bounds."[19]

Gross discussed only the propriety of Brandeis's financial arrangement with Frankfurter. The arrangement, wrote Gross, "was something that would have been frowned upon if it had been known to the public. A judge, especially a Supreme Court Justice, was expected to sit high on the bench and interpret the law. The fact that other judges engaged in the same kind of activity does not alter the fact that Brandeis's actions, from a strictly legal and ethical view, were questionable."[20]

In summary, the biographies after Mason's contain the following charges of impropriety against Brandeis:

1. Participating in the drafting of a politically partisan document.

2. Threatening to hold legislation unconstitutional if the executive branch did not follow his policy views.

3. Providing Frankfurter with a regular stipend for political activities to accomplish Brandeis's policy goals.

4. Immersing himself in the formulation of executive and legislative policy.

Before considering the propriety of Brandeis's extrajudicial activity, it is necessary to discuss the standards used for making such determinations. Several standards have been used in determining the propriety of extrajudicial activity—canons of judicial ethics, collective judicial prescriptions, individual judicial prescriptions, public expectations, precedent, and conscience.

In 1924, eight years after Brandeis's appointment to the Supreme Court, the American Bar Association adopted its first code of judicial ethics. The most specific provision in the code dealing with extrajudicial activity was a canon that acknowledged that a judge is entitled to entertain political views and have the same rights as other citizens. But, the code added, "it is inevitable that suspicion of being warped by political bias will attach to a judge who becomes the active promoter of the interests of one political party as against another. He should avoid making political speeches, making or soliciting payment of assessments or contributions to party funds, the

public endorsement of candidates for political office and participation in party conventions."[21] Other canons plausibly related to extrajudicial activity were more general. The official
conduct of judges should be "free from impropriety and the
appearance of impropriety," and their conduct in everyday
life "should be beyond reproach";[22] judges should do nothing
that would "justify the impression" that others might influence their impartiality;[23] and judges should be careful to avoid
actions that would "awaken suspicion" that their business
relations or friendships influenced their judicial conduct.[24]
Although the canons lack precision, taken together, they suggest that it is improper for judges to do anything that affects
their impartiality or gives the appearance of doing so.

During Brandeis's tenure on the Supreme Court, its members collectively agreed on standards of propriety that were
more specific than the 1924 canons. The major collective prescriptions were as follows:

1. No justice should be involved in any activity that even
hints of corruption.[25]

2. No justice should participate in an electoral campaign.[26]

3. No justice should give advice to another branch of government in any matter that is likely to come before the Supreme Court.[27]

4. No justice should speak publicly on any matter that is
likely to come before the Supreme Court.[28]

5. No justice should give advice on executive appoint-
ments unless requested to do so.[29]

These prescriptions reflect a concern for avoiding extrajudicial activity that might affect impartiality or give the appearance of affecting impartiality. To a lesser extent, they also
reflect a concern for separation of powers.

Individual justices often hold prescriptions concerning
extrajudicial activity that are more or less restrictive than the
collective prescriptions of their colleagues. Brandeis's personal code of propriety was especially stringent: no honorary
degrees, no writing of articles, no speeches, no investments
that could even remotely cause a conflict of interest, no un-
invited contacts with other branches of government, no ex-

tensive involvement in social causes. Mason quoted Justice Harlan F. Stone as saying that Brandeis "was strongly of the belief that a Justice of the Court should devote himself single-mindedly to his duties as a Justice, without undertaking to engage in any outside activities."[30] Although Brandeis occasionally violated his own prescriptions, some of those departures—for example, a speech on a matter not likely to come before the Court—do not raise any question of impropriety.[31]

Public expectation of propriety is a difficult standard to apply because it is usually vague and changes over time. Yet the standard is important because there is general agreement that if the justices violate it, they undermine the Supreme Court's legitimacy.[32] But one must be wary of retroactive application of the standard. As Paper pointed out, questionable extrajudicial activity must be judged in the context of the time in which it occurred.

The standard of precedent—what has been done may be done—has serious problems because justices have often acted contrary to their collective and individual prescriptions. Thus, practically all extrajudicial activity, including questionable activity, can be justified by precedent. At best, precedent is a suspect standard for determining the propriety of extrajudicial activity.

Conscience is the ultimate standard for justices who plan to engage in extrajudicial activity. Justices may consider canons of judicial ethics, collective and individual judicial prescriptions, public expectations, and precedent, but only their individual consciences can dictate their conduct in specific instances. At times, conscience may even require extrajudicial conduct that appears ethically questionable.[33] Conscience-based extrajudicial activity is, I believe, entitled to the benefit of doubt, for justices are appointed to the Supreme Court for their ethical sensitivity as well as their legal expertise. Yet conscience as a standard of propriety is not without problems. I believe the standard is acceptable for determining propriety "only when conscience is informed by a sensitive understanding of the judicial function and the separation of powers. Such a sensitive conscience would forswear not only conduct that would affect a justice's impartiality in the decision of cases, but even conduct that gives the appearance that impartiality might be affected."[34] This standard captures the essence of the relevant 1924 canons and the justices' collective prescriptions during Brandeis's tenure on the Supreme Court. In addition, it is useful in determining whether individual justices' prescriptions are too scrupulous or not scrupulous enough, whether public expectations of propriety are too high or too low, and whether precedents may be used in measuring extrajudicial activity. If extrajudicial activity affects impartiality, it is improper. If it gives the appearance of affecting impartiality, then it is at least ethically questionable.[35]

Although the requirements of proof are not the same in history as they are in law, I believe that judicial impropriety must be proven by primary evidence that is clear and convincing. So the first question in this inquiry is whether such evidence shows that the conduct asserted as improper occurred. If it does, the next question is whether that conduct violates an acceptable standard of propriety. These are the questions I shall attempt to answer in discussing the four charges of impropriety that others have made against Brandeis.

Participation in Drafting a Partisan Document

There is no doubt that Brandeis helped to draft a partisan document at Wilson's request in the early twenties. Although such action was not without precedent, it violated Brandeis's personal code of propriety, the prescriptions of his colleagues, and perhaps also the 1924 canons. Although Mason had discerned no impropriety in the matter, Urofsky and others have concluded that Brandeis acted contrary to public expectations of propriety. They may be right, but that is difficult to prove. Brandeis appears not to have acted in violation of his conscience. On the one hand, there were the claims of friendship and honor to grant the request of an ailing and broken ex-president who had appointed him to the Supreme Court; on the other hand, there was the claim of duty not to act in a way that would injure the Court's reputation. He resolved the conflicting claims by participating discreetly and confidentially in drafting the partisan platform. There is no evidence that his activity affected his impartiality in the decision of any case, but his activity was so clearly political that, if disclosed, it would have given the appearance of affecting his impartiality. For that reason, I believe that activity must be viewed as ethically questionable.

Threatening to Hold Legislation Unconstitutional

Murphy's assertion in 1982 that Brandeis had threatened to declare New Deal legislation unconstitutional if the Roosevelt administration did not follow his policy views is the most serious charge of impropriety against Brandeis, for if supported by the evidence, it constitutes "malfeasance, perhaps worthy of impeachment."[36] Here is Murphy's assertion and supporting evidence.

> Finally exasperated, in late April 1934, Brandeis decided that the time for patient teaching combined with occasional urgent warnings had passed. Now was the time for nothing short of overt threats. Through Gardner Jackson, the justice sent a message to Rexford Tugwell and Jerome Frank that "he was declaring war" on the New Deal. Though Tugwell was not moved by Brandeis's vision of the AAA, such a threat from a member of the Supreme Court caused great consternation. So he passed the message along directly to President Roosevelt, who promised to see Brandeis as soon as possible to "butter him up some." According to Tugwell's account, the administration took this warning so seriously that Jerome Frank "succeeded in postponing the prosecution of an oil code case . . . on the theory that with Brandeis feeling as he does we ought not to take the case up."
>
> A previously unpublished exchange of letters discovered in FDR's personal files at Hyde Park show [sic] how far the desperate, aging justice was willing to go in playing political hardball with the president. Knowing that

all his indications of displeasure would find their way
back to the Oval Office, Brandeis also lectured Jerome
Frank and Adolf A. Berle on the issue of "bigness." This
time, though, the justice's critical assessment of the
AAA and the NRA was followed by an unmistakable
warning—which Berle immediately forwarded to Roosevelt—that Brandeis *had gone along with the legislation
up to now, but that unless he could see some reversal of the
big business trend, he was disposed to hold the government
control legislation unconstitutional from then on.*[37]

The italicized portion of the statement is from a letter writ-
ten by Berle to Roosevelt on April 23, 1934, which Murphy
cited. Murphy gave the impression in this passage that
Berle and Frank had heard Brandeis make the threat and that
Berle then reported to FDR what he had heard Brandeis say.
The evidence that Murphy cited does not, however, support
that interpretation. Here is the full text of Berle's letter to
FDR.

                                        April 23, 1934
Dear Caesar:
    Mr. Justice Brandeis has been revolving matters in his
head and I think requires some attention. At all events,
he stated his view to Jerome Frank the other evening,
asking to see me and Rexford Tugwell. His idea was that
we were steadily creating organisms of big business
which were growing in power, wiping out the middle
class, eliminating small business and putting themselves
in a place in which they rather than the government were
controlling the nation's destinies. He added that he had
gone along with the legislation to now; but that unless
he could see some reversal of the big business trend, he
was disposed to hold the government control legislation
unconstitutional from now on. I think also he regretted
not having had a chance to talk to you about it. He, of
course, wants drastic taxation of big business units, accompanied by leaving small business, via the N.R.A.,
strictly alone.

His view, if ever stated, would command wide popular support. But as long as people want Ford cars they
are likely to have Ford factories and finance to match.
I am, as always,

Faithfully yours,
s/ ADOLF A. BERLE[38]

The letter reports not what Brandeis told Berle but what Berle
thought Brandeis said to Frank. Thus, Berle's statement is
hearsay. It may even be double or triple hearsay, for on April
26, 1934, Tugwell wrote in his diary: "The other day, Brandeis
sent word, in effect, that he was declaring war. It came
through Gardner Jackson to Jerry Frank and myself."[39] If Tugwell and Berle were referring to the same remarks attributed
to Brandeis—and given the dates and content of the two documents that seems to be the case—Brandeis gave his views to
Jackson, who reported them to Tugwell and Frank, who
passed them on to Berle, who then relayed them to FDR. Such
evidence, in my view, cannot be relied upon to support a
serious charge of judicial impropriety. Thus, Murphy's conclusion that Brandeis threatened to hold legislation unconstitutional cannot be accepted as fact.[40]

Unless new direct evidence surfaces on the matter, the
verdict of history is likely to be that Brandeis was perhaps
imprudent in expressing his criticisms of the New Deal to
members of the executive branch but not that he abused the
powers of his judicial office by threatening to declare legislation unconstitutional if the administration did not follow his
views.[41]

The Brandeis-Frankfurter Financial Arrangement

There is solid evidence showing that Brandeis supported
Frankfurter's political activities with an annual stipend for
many years, but that evidence does not convincingly prove
Murphy's interpretation of the character, purpose, and extent
of the arrangement. That interpretation, upon which the *New
York Times* relied in concluding that the arrangement "was
wrong,"[42] rests essentially on three assertions.

Murphy's first assertion was that the arrangement was conceived from the beginning—that is, 1916—as "a long-term lobbying effort" in which Frankfurter would be Brandeis's "paid political lobbyist and lieutenant."[43] But the only evidence Murphy cited bearing on Brandeis's intentions at the time were two letters written to Frankfurter in 1916. In the first, Brandeis wrote:

> My Dear Felix: You have had considerable expense for travelling, telephoning and similar expenses in public matters undertaken at my request or following up my suggestions & will have more in the future no doubt. These expenses should, of course, be borne by me.
>
> I am sending check for $250 on this account. Let me know when it is exhausted or if it has already been.[44]

When Frankfurter answered that he appreciated the gesture but could not accept the check, Brandeis wrote to him again.

> My Dear Felix: Alice and I talked over the matter before I sent the check and considered it again carefully on receipt of your letter. We are clearly of opinion that you ought to take the check.
>
> In essence this is nothing different than your taking travelling and incidental expenses from the Consumers League or the New Republic—which I trust you do. You are giving your very valuable time and that is quite enough. It can make no difference that the subject matter in connection with which expense is incurred is more definite in one case than in the other.
>
> I ought to feel free to make suggestions to you, although they involved some incidental expense. And you should feel free to incur expense in the public interest. So I am returning the check.[45]

The letters do not support the interpretation that Brandeis and Frankfurter envisioned "a long-term lobbying effort." Brandeis did not specify the nature of the activities for which Frankfurter's expenses would be paid; he said only that those activities were to be "in the public interest." Further, practically all of Brandeis's requests to Frankfurter from 1916 to 1920 that Murphy reports concerned Zionist activities. Thus, the most plausible interpretation of the Brandeis-Frankfurter arrangement's purpose, at least until the twenties, is the one that Urofsky and Levy gave in 1975: "LDB set up an expense fund for Frankfurter's use, so that the law school professor would not have to bear the costs of his Zionist work."[46]

Murphy's second assertion was that Brandeis made annual payments to Frankfurter from 1916 to 1938 and that the amounts increased as the expenses of their political activities rose. Murphy stated, "In mid-1917 [Brandeis] placed $1,000 in the special account, and then replenished that amount in each of the next seven years."[47] In 1925, according to Murphy, Frankfurter received $1,500, and thereafter, until 1938, he received $3,500 per year.[48]

The letters Murphy cited, however, show a different picture. In 1917 Brandeis had sent Frankfurter a check for $1,000 as a contribution to a memorial fund for a friend who had died. When arrangements for the fund were delayed, Brandeis asked Frankfurter to deposit the check "in a special account & draw against it for your disbursements, past & future, in public matters."[49] None of the documents Murphy cited shows payment by Brandeis to Frankfurter between 1917 and 1922. In 1922 Brandeis told Judge Julian W. Mack that he would send Frankfurter a check for $1,000.[50] This discussion was in the context of paying for Frankfurter's expenses in Zionist affairs. In 1923 Brandeis wrote Frankfurter and said that he planned to send a check for $1,000 to defray Frankfurter's disbursements in public affairs,[51] "unless you and Marion [Frankfurter's wife] object."[52]

In 1925 Frankfurter wrote Brandeis about a personal financial problem.[53] Two years earlier his wife had suffered a nervous breakdown, and therapy required an additional annual expenditure of $1,500. He told Brandeis he could make that amount easily doing odd jobs for New York lawyer friends, but he begrudged the time it would take from intrinsically more important work. The following was Brandeis's response: "I am glad you wrote me about the personal needs and I'll send the $1,500 now or in installments as you may prefer. Your public service must not be abridged. Marion knows that Alice and I look upon you as half brother, half son."[54]

This evidence tends to negate the existence of any regular financial connection before October 1925; payments from Brandeis to Frankfurter up to that time were *ad hoc* and represented reimbursement for expenditures already made. It was only beginning in late 1925 that Brandeis consistently made payments to Frankfurter of $3,500 per year—usually $2,000 in January and $1,500 in October; there were also occasional additional payments for special projects.[55]

The wills of Louis and Alice Brandeis, which Murphy apparently failed to examine, reinforce an interpretation, suggested by the above letter, that the stipend had the dual purpose of advancing the public good and helping a close friend in need. The principal legatees in Mrs. Brandeis's will were her daughters, Susan and Elizabeth, and Frankfurter; each was to receive $50,000. Mrs. Brandeis also provided generously for other relatives and friends, but none was to receive more than $25,000. Justice Brandeis's own will at the time also ranked Frankfurter among relatives, and Frankfurter was the only person in the will whom Brandeis designated "my friend." Brandeis gave Frankfurter the same percentage of his estate as he gave his brother, Alfred, his nephew, Louis B. Wehle, and his wife's sisters, Pauline and Josephine Goldmark, and made all of the gifts for the same purpose: "to enable them the more freely to devote time to the public service."[56] In addition, both Louis and Alice Brandeis characterized payments of Frankfurter's stipend as gifts.

Murphy's third assertion was that the arrangement was secret, that is, deliberately hidden from public view.[57] He provided no evidence for this assertion. Instead, he argued that the stipend was secret because he could find nothing to indicate either that Brandeis's colleagues on the Supreme Court knew of the arrangement or that any other person except Judge Mack knew of it.[58] But even if Brandeis did not tell his colleagues on the Court of the stipend, that fact does not necessarily imply that he was hiding it. Certainly, his failure to disclose his simultaneous contributions to various educational institutions, causes, friends, and relatives did not suggest that he was hiding those contributions.[59] None of the documents mentioning the payments to Frankfurter indicates that the arrangement was secret. Further, there is evidence that persons other than Mack knew that Brandeis had been helping Frankfurter financially.[60]

Thus, the arrangement was not, as Murphy suggests, sinister. But it is true that Brandeis told Frankfurter in 1927 that the stipend was being paid to him "for our joint endeavors through you."[61] And some of those endeavors involved matters likely to come before the Supreme Court.[62] Thus, even though the evidence does not convincingly prove Murphy's assertions in their entirety, it does raise a serious question about the propriety of the Brandeis-Frankfurter arrangement.

The arrangement was unprecedented. Chief Justice William H. Taft sometimes used intermediaries for political purposes, but that was done *ad hoc* and involved no payment.[63] So precedent as a standard provides no clear answer to the question of propriety. Nor do judicial collective prescriptions, for there was no prescription concerning the matter. It appears that the arrangement did not violate Brandeis's individual prescriptions. His personal code of propriety concerning his assistance to Frankfurter was apparently the same as for his activity concerning Zionism—that he do no more than "(1) to think on the main problems of the cause; (2) to give moral support; and (3) to give financial support."[64] It also appears that the arrangement was not a violation of conscience, for apparently Brandeis's motives were to help a friend in need and at the same time advance the public good.

Brandeis may have violated the public-expectation standard in his financial arrangement with Frankfurter. The *New York Times*'s strong negative reaction to the arrangement in 1982 provides some support for that view, but it must be remembered that the *Times*'s reaction was based on Murphy's exaggerated account of the matter and that public expectations of judicial propriety were stricter in the eighties than they were in the twenties and thirties. Although Brandeis's impartiality never seems to have been compromised and his payments to Frankfurter apparently never affected the decision of any case,[65] such conduct creating the appearance of a possible compromise of impartiality raises questions of impropriety. I do not conclude, as the *Times* did, that the Brandeis-Frankfurter financial relationship was "wrong," but I do believe it was ethically questionable.

Immersion in the Formulation of Policy

Finally, Strum's conclusion that Brandeis had immersed himself in the formulation of legislative policy "in a most unjudicial manner" is supported by clear and convincing primary evidence.[66] Strum focused particularly on Brandeis's activity during the New Deal. Her best example was Brandeis's involvement in formulating and enacting the unemployment insurance provisions of the Social Security Act of 1935. That involvement began in the summer of 1933. Brandeis, his daughter Elizabeth, and her husband Paul Raushenbush discussed how federal legislation might be used to encourage the states to provide unemployment compensation. "Have you considered," asked Brandeis, "the case of *Florida* v. *Mellon*?" Slowly they grasped the point of his question: The case provided constitutional justification for legislation they wanted. *Florida* v. *Mellon* had upheld a federal law that permitted the use of state inheritance taxes as a credit against federal inheritance taxes.[67] On September 16, 1933, Brandeis wrote his daughter Elizabeth setting forth his views for a national unemployment insurance plan. "F.D. [Roosevelt]," Brandeis wrote, "indicated to F.F. [Frankfurter] a desire to talk with me generally on matters, before Court convenes. If he carries out his purpose, I want to discuss irregularity of employment with him. Let me have as soon as possible your & Paul's views as to the above; &, if you can, a rough suggestion for a bill."[68] Brandeis then formulated a plan based on *Florida* v. *Mellon*; he suggested "a federal payroll tax on employers, from which they could deduct whatever amount they were paying into state unemployment plans."[69] Later in the fall the Raushenbushes met with Charles Wyzanski, Tom Corcoran, and other young New Dealers and liberal business leaders to discuss Brandeis's plan.[70] During the Christmas holidays, they met with A. Lincoln Filene, Frances Perkins, and Sen. Robert A. Wagner to organize a campaign "in support of the Brandeis idea."[71] When Roosevelt decided to delay consideration of the bill, Brandeis saw the president about the matter. In a letter marked "Strictly Confidential," Brandeis wrote to his daughter Elizabeth: "Don't be discouraged by the President's message. He summoned me yesterday & when I reached him at 4:45 P.M. he had in his hands his message & started to read it to me. When he came to the part on social insurance, I stopped him, told him it was all wrong, & for about 3/4 hour discussed that question & I think I convinced him of the error. He said the message had already gone to the Capitol & it was too late to change that; but it would not commit him to means, etc. I have left some efficient friends in Washington, who are to work for the true faith during the summer."[72] Congress enacted the bill, and the president signed it on August 15, 1935.

Brandeis's advice to FDR violated neither the standards of precedent nor conscience. Other justices had given similar advice to presidents and cabinet members, and there is little doubt that Brandeis believed he had acted properly.[73] But it did violate the justices' collective prescription, as well as Brandeis's own prescription, against giving advice in a matter likely to come before the Court, and Strum apparently thought it had violated the public-expectation standard.[74] William O. Douglas, however, believed that Brandeis's advising of presidents on policy was not improper, for if it "caused any collision with future judicial decisions . . . , [Brandeis] would have been the first to suggest that [he] not sit."[75] But Brandeis did not disqualify himself when the constitutionality of the unemployment compensation insurance program was challenged in *Stewart Machine Co.* v. *Davis*,[76] and the Court upheld the program by a five-to-four vote.

Was Brandeis's participation in *Stewart Machine Co.* v. *Davis* improper? Under the 1924 canons, it would have been if his conduct gave the appearance of impropriety.[77] His participation appears to have violated the collective prescriptions of at least some of his colleagues in the thirties.[78] But precedent can be cited for Brandeis's participation in the case.[79] Presumably, Brandeis's failure to disqualify himself did not violate his conscience, and there is no evidence that his impartiality had been compromised. However, his participation in the case showed an insensitivity to the separation of powers and gave the appearance that his impartiality might be affected, for Brandeis had formulated the legislation, indicated that he thought it was constitutional, encouraged others to support it, and advised the president to enact it. Further, at Brandeis's request, Frankfurter had supported the legislation in both the White House and Congress while receiving a regular stipend from Brandeis for such activities.[80] Thus, Brandeis's participation in *Stewart Machine Co.* v. *Davis* appears to have been at least ethically questionable.[81]

This inquiry suggests the following observations:

First, I doubt that Brandeis ever thought his extrajudicial activity was improper. His sense of rectitude was extraordinary. I do not agree with the suggestion of the *New York Times* that Brandeis was morally arrogant.[82] Morally autonomous is a better description. Frankfurter once wrote that Brandeis "had the utmost attainable intellectual and moral autonomy."[83] Brandeis's primary standard for action was his own conscience. If he believed he was right, that settled the matter for him, no matter what others might think. Lewis Paper agrees. In a letter written after the publication of his biography of Brandeis, Paper wrote that "Brandeis had an incredible self-confidence that blinded him to ethical considerations that might have deterred another attorney. . . . He was so sure of himself, so convinced of the purity of his dedication to the public interest, that he could not see conflicts that seem so obvious to the outside."[84]

Second, Brandeis deeply respected the Court as an institution; thus, he tried to avoid activity that would negatively affect its reputation. That was the reason for his quiet, confidential, discreet, behind-the-scenes approach when he acted extrajudicially. The event that underlay his approach was a public address he made at a Zionist meeting in New York in 1916, less than two months after his appointment to the Supreme Court. His opponents openly attacked him at the meeting. One of them shook his finger at Brandeis saying that the Jewish people would repudiate him. Another cried out, "There are higher things than the Supreme Court of the United States!"[85] Two days later, the *New York Times* censured Brandeis for participating publicly in the controversial meeting. As a justice, said the *Times*, Brandeis had an obligation "to withdraw from any activities of a political or social nature . . . and avoid all controversies or commitments which might seem in any degree to affect their judicial impartiality of mind."[86] Stung by the double attack, Brandeis resigned his formal positions in the Zionist movement. "If I were a private citizen, and concerned only personally," he told a fellow Zionist, "I should, for the sake of our cause, ignore the attack, as I did so many times in the past in the course of other public work. But I feel that respect for the high Court, of which I am a member, and therefore also the future of our cause, demands that so far as humanly possible I should guard against the repetition of such events."[87] And he did. Brandeis's reaction to the attacks for the New York address in 1916 appears to be the origin of his personal prescription against public speeches and his *sub rosa* approach to extrajudicial activities, including his financial arrangement with Frankfurter.

Third, Brandeis's questionable extrajudicial activity will not significantly diminish his place in history. He will remain the modern hero originally portrayed in Mason's biography. To some, he will be a hero with chinks in his armor. To others, he will be a misunderstood prophet. To his successors on the Supreme Court, the ethical problems raised by his off-the-bench political conduct will quite likely be a lesson in the perils of such conduct.

---

1. Alpheus T. Mason, *Brandeis: A Free Man's Life* (New York: Viking Press, 1946).

2. Ibid., 566, 584, 597, 602, 617.

3. Ibid., 451-64, 518-29, 533-36, 566-67, 586-88, 593-97, 603-6.

4. Ibid., 521-22.

5. Ibid., 522.

6. Ibid. Apparently, it never occurred to Brandeis nor to those close to him that the propriety of his advice to Wilson might be questioned. On April 20, 1918, Mrs. Brandeis described the meeting to her sister, Susan Goldmark. "You know his [LDB's] study. It is not a very large room and now lined with bookshelves on all sides from floor to ceiling. The room was fairly dark, with only one strong desk light. He had been working at some opinion, consulting authorities, and law books were lying everywhere about—on his desk, on chairs, even on the floor. . . . Here surely was the scholar, the student at his work. And yet it is as a practical man of affairs, a statesman, that Louis's advice is so much sought" (ibid.).

7. Ibid., 534.

8. Ibid., 533-36.

9. Ibid., 535.

10. Melvin I. Urofsky, *A Mind of One Piece: Brandeis and American Reform* (New York: Scribner's, 1971), 138.

11. Bruce Allen Murphy, *The Brandeis/Frankfurter Connection: The Secret Political Activities of Two Supreme Court Justices* (New York: Oxford Univ. Press, 1982).

12. *New York Times*, Feb. 14, 1982, 1; Feb. 18, 1982, A22.

13. Lewis J. Paper, *Brandeis* (Englewood Cliffs, N.J.: Prentice-Hall, 1983); Philippa Strum, *Louis D. Brandeis: Justice for the People* (Cambridge, Mass.: Harvard Univ. Press, 1984); Leonard Baker, *Brandeis and Frankfurter: A Dual Biography* (New York: Harper & Row, 1984); David C. Gross, *A Justice for All the People: Louis D. Brandeis* (New York: E.P. Dutton, 1987).

14. Paper, *Brandeis*, 290.

15. Ibid., 257.

16. Strum, *Brandeis*, 219-20, 403.

17. Ibid., 404.

18. Baker, *Brandeis and Frankfurter*, 197.

19. Ibid., 243-44, 304-6.

20. Gross, *A Justice for All the People*, 81-82.

21. Canon 28, Canons of Judicial Ethics, American Bar Association, *Report of the Forty-seventh Annual Meeting* (Baltimore: Lord Baltimore Press, 1924), 768.

22. Canon 4, ibid., 762.

23. Canon 13, ibid., 764.

24. Canon 33, ibid., 769.

25. William J. Cibes, Jr., "Extra-Judicial Activities of Justices of the United States Supreme Court, 1790-1960" (Unpublished Ph.D. diss., Princeton University, 1975), 1114.

26. Ibid., 1104, 1394, 1420. For the period from 1888 to 1921, Cibes reported that "overt electoral action by Justices" was proscribed. "Even those who failed to conform to the strict standards of their colleagues," he added, "nevertheless indicated that they believed the *prima facie* rule to bar such action; such political actions would be taken only in extreme circumstances, and only with reluctance" (1104). For the period from 1921 to 1960, Cibes wrote: "Almost all justices concluded that participating in electoral politics was activity in which members of the Court ought not to engage. Politicking might injure the reputation of the Court—and might indeed bias a Justice's decisions" (1394).

27. Ibid., 1116, 1393, 1442.

28. Ibid., 1111.

29. Ibid., 1393.

30. Quoted in Mason, *Brandeis*, 584. See also Strum, *Brandeis*, 372.

31. Strum, however, believed that Brandeis must be held to his own stern ethical code because he had imposed it "on himself and judged others by it" (ibid., 402).

32. Strum made a strong argument for the thesis that the Supreme Court's legitimacy will be undermined if justices act contrary to the myth that the Court and its members are apolitical (ibid., 402-3). Cibes disagreed. He argued that "just as the Court survived the advent of judicial realism, which destroyed mechanical jurisprudence, the Court will survive the truth about the extent of extrajudicial activity" ("Extra-Judicial Activities of Justices," 1504-5).

33. See Walter F. Murphy, *The Elements of Judicial Strategy* (Chicago: Univ. of Chicago Press, 1964), 196-97.

34. David J. Danelski, "Brandeis and Frankfurter," *Harvard Law Review* 96 (1982): 330.

35. I make a distinction between extrajudicial activity that affects impartiality and extrajudicial activity that gives the appearance of doing so in determining propriety because it is difficult to assess the effect of the latter on the public generally. Russell R. Wheeler appropriately asks: "Must we assume without question that extrajudicial activity, even if it does not corrupt the judicial function, must be abandoned because it has 'the appearance of impropriety'?" My answer is no, but, as Wheeler suggests, it is appropriate to question such activity. *Extrajudicial Behavior and the Role of the Supreme Court Justice* (Morristown: General Learning Press, 1975), 16.

36. Philip Kurland, " 'Brandeis-Frankfurter' Sensationalizes Serious Issues," *Legal Times*, April 12, 1982, 10.

37. Murphy, *Brandeis/Frankfurter Connection*, 140-41.

38. Berle to Roosevelt, F.D. Roosevelt Papers, FDR Library, Box PPF 1306.
39. Rexford Tugwell Diaries, April 26, 1934, Rexford Tugwell Papers, FDR Library, Box 16. Here is the Tugwell statement in context.

The other day Brandeis sent word, in effect, that he was declaring war. It came through Gardner Jackson to Jerry Frank and myself. He, of course, does not believe the government ought to try to do so much as it is now trying to do. He believes in small enterprises, competing freely—all that goes with the familiar "free competition." In a way policy up to now has been a compromise between the old "honesty in business" principle that he approves—the securities act, the stock exchange act, the food and drug bill, etc.—and recognition and control of the trend toward large scale machine processes, together with an enlargement of government functions. This last he is against. Tom Corcoran, who is sincere, adroit, and a little of a schemer, represents his point of view. So does Landis to a less degree. There are no differences here we cannot compromise. We need a good deal of regulation in the decades to come; but it is important to get a real start in overhead planning and government ownership. The development will necessarily be slow and will be inefficient at first, but it must go on.

I called in Ernest Lindley and asked him to get at Corcoran and after Cabinet yesterday (H.A.W. being in Nebraska making a speech) asked F.D.R. to get hold of Brandeis and butter him some. He said he would. Jerry Frank also succeeded in postponing the prosecution of an oil code case in conference with all the big-shot lawyers on the theory that with Brandeis feeling as he does we ought not to take the case up. Ickes was inclined to be indignant (the oil administration is under him) so I told him about Brandeis's activation. He said he hadn't realized that the old justice was so intransigent. I think few people do; but it is so, and Jerry and I have seemed to fail in working on him. Frankfurter shares his prejudices but doesn't feel so strongly about it. I think we could compromise with him.

40. Baker, who maintained that Brandeis committed no serious impropriety in any of his extrajudicial activity, accepted the threat as fact. "At times Brandeis," wrote Baker, "grumbled to his friends. He vowed to Jerome Frank that he would vote against New Deal

proposals on the Court" (Baker, *Brandeis and Frankfurter*, 301). Baker cited Berle's letter to FDR, April 23, 1933, as support for his statement.

41. See Michael Parrish, *Felix Frankfurter and His Times* (New York: Free Press, 1982), 261-62; Arthur M. Schlesinger, Jr., *The Politics of Upheaval* (Boston: Houghton Mifflin, 1960), 280.

42. *New York Times*, Feb. 18, 1982, A22. The reanalysis of the primary materials used by Murphy to support his interpretation of the Brandeis-Frankfurter arrangement that follows was initially published in my review of *The Brandeis/Frankfurter Connection*, "Brandeis and Frankfurter," 312-30.

43. Murphy, *Brandeis/Frankfurter Connection*, 10, 40.

44. Melvin I. Urofsky and David W. Levy, eds., *The Letters of Louis D. Brandeis*, 5 vols. (Albany: State Univ. of New York Press 1971-), 4:266 (abbreviated hereafter as BL).

45. Brandeis to Frankfurter, Nov. 25, 1916, BL, 4:266-67.

46. Ibid., 4:458.

47. Murphy, *Brandeis/Frankfurter Connection*, 41.

48. Ibid., 41-42.

49. Brandeis to Frankfurter, May 3, 1917, Felix Frankfurter Papers, Library of Congress (abbreviated hereafter as FP).

50. Brandeis to Mack, Jan. 12, 1922, BL, 4:458.

51. Brandeis to Frankfurter, Jan. 3, 1923; Jan. 6, 1923, FP.

52. Ibid.

53. Quoted in H.N. Hirsch, *The Enigma of Felix Frankfurter* (New York: Basic Books, 1981), 225. Frankfurter's letter to Brandeis was undated.

54. Brandeis to Frankfurter, Sept. 24, 1925, BL, 5:187.

55. Brandeis to Frankfurter, Oct. 2, 1925; Dec. 27, 1925; June 5, 1927; Aug. 16, 1927; April 11, 1929; July 30, 1934, FP.

56. The Brandeis wills are in the Louis D. Brandeis Papers, University of Louisville Archives (abbreviated hereafter as BP). They are available on microfilm through interlibrary loan. For more details on the wills, see Danelski, "Brandeis and Frankfurter," 321-22.

57. Murphy, *Brandeis/Frankfurter Connection*, 11, 12, 44, 145.

58. Brandeis had mentioned the matter twice to Mack—once in 1922 and again in 1934—and both times in the context of paying Frankfurter's expenses for Zionist affairs. In the second letter, Brandeis stated that he had for years paid Frankfurter a stipend of $3,500 per year for public purposes (Brandeis to Mack, March 11, 1934, BP).

59. For a tabulation of Brandeis's contributions by year, see Mason, *Brandeis*, 692.

60. See Brandeis to Jacob de Haas, April 7, 1922, BL, 4:458; Robert M. Cover, "The Framing of Justice Brandeis," *New Republic*, May 5, 1982, 20; Strum, *Brandeis*, 374-75, 475; Baker, *Brandeis and Frankfurter*, 244.

61. Brandeis to Frankfurter, June 2, 1927, BL, 5:290.

62. The best example was Frankfurter's activity, at Brandeis's request, to further the passage of the unemployment compensation insurance provisions of the Social Security Act. This matter will be considered in the next section of this paper.

63. See David J. Danelski, *A Supreme Court Justice Is Appointed* (New York: Random House, 1964), 67-70.

64. Brandeis to de Haas, March 28, 1928, quoted in Mason, *Brandeis*, 593.

65. Murphy argued, however, that Brandeis's payments to Frankfurter may have affected Brandeis's behavior in the Sacco and Vanzetti case. Brandeis disqualified himself in the case apparently because a member of his household, Mrs. Glendower Evans, known as "Auntie B.," had been actively involved in defense efforts for Sacco and Vanzetti. Frankfurter was similarly involved, and Brandeis offered to contribute an additional sum to Frankfurter for his incidental expenses in the case; Brandeis later contributed $500, apparently for that purpose (Brandeis to Frankfurter, June 2, 1927; Aug. 16, 1927, FP). When lawyers for Sacco and Vanzetti called on Brandeis to request a stay of execution on Aug. 21, 1927, Brandeis refused to see them, because he believed that personal connections with the case required his disqualification.

66. Strum, *Brandeis*, 404.

67. Nelson L. Dawson, *Louis D. Brandeis, Felix Frankfurter, and the New Deal* (Hamden, Conn.: Archon Books, 1980), 105.

68. Quoted in Strum, *Brandeis*, 386.

69. Ibid.

70. Ibid. Strum did not say where this meeting was held. Freedman wrote that strategy meetings and drafting sessions for the unemployment compensation insurance legislation "were often held in Brandeis's apartment, with Frankfurter present and very active" (*Roosevelt and Frankfurter: Their Correspondence, 1928-1945* [Boston and Toronto: Little, Brown & Co., 1967], 226).

71. Strum, *Brandeis*, 387. According to Strum, Filene arranged the meeting. Paper described the meeting as occurring in early Jan. 1934 at Filene's daughter's home. According to Paper, Brandeis had arranged the meeting (*Brandeis*, 355).

72. Brandeis to Elizabeth Raushenbush, June 8, 1934, quoted in

Strum, *Brandeis*, 386. Reporting on the bill to Frankfurter, Corcoran wrote on June 18, 1934, "[Some New Dealers] did their bit toward shelving Isaiah's unemployment insurance bill at this session as too tame" (Freedman, *Roosevelt and Frankfurter*, 224).

73. The most striking precedent for the giving of advisory opinions occurred in 1872 during Salmon P. Chase's chief justiceship. That precedent is interesting in this context because it touches a matter considered by Murphy and Strum—Brandeis's ability to separate sufficiently his advisory role from his judicial role and thus to justify not only sitting in cases dealing with matters on which he had given advice but also voting against legislation that he had earlier supported (see Murphy, *Brandeis/Frankfurter Connection*, 55, 142; Strum, *Brandeis*, 404). Asked for an opinion by Secretary of State Hamilton Fish about the constitutionality of certain provisions of a proposed treaty, Chief Justice Chase replied that there was no impropriety in Fish's request or in his own response. He told Fish that he had consulted his two senior colleagues and they all thought one provision was unconstitutional but were divided on the constitutionality of another. Chase, however, cautioned Fish, "These impressions may, of course, be changed upon argument and full consideration, should questions involving them ever be brought before us for judicial decision" (Salmon P. Chase to Hamilton Fish, Dec. 10, 1872, Salmon P. Chase Papers, Library of Congress).

74. Strum, *Brandeis*, 403.

75. William O. Douglas, *The Court Years* (New York: Random House, 1975), 253.

76. 301 U.S. 548 (1937).

77. See Canon 4.

78. Justices Owen Roberts and Hugo Black informed William O. Douglas that they thought he would have to disqualify himself in all cases that "bore directly or indirectly" on matters he worked on in the executive branch during the summer of 1942. Douglas agreed, and partly for that reason he declined FDR's invitation to work on war contracts in the executive branch that summer (Douglas to FDR [draft], June 1942, William O. Douglas Papers, Library of Congress, Box 367).

79. Chief Justice Chase participated in the decision of the legal tender cases, which involved fiscal policy he had formulated as secretary of the treasury. *Hepburn* vs. *Georgia*, 8 Wall. 603 (U.S. 1890); *Legal Tender Cases*, 12 Wall. 457 (U.S. 1891). See John P. Frank, "Disqualification of Judges," 56 *Yale Law Journal* 625 (1947).

80. Dawson, *Brandeis, Frankfurter, and The New Deal*, 109-10;

Freedman, *Roosevelt and Frankfurter*, 224; Parrish, *Felix Frankfurter and His Times*, 247-48.

81. Brandeis's failure to disqualify himself in *Stewart Machine Co. v. Davis* appears to have been a rare instance of such conduct on his part. He disqualified himself in the Sacco and Vanzetti and Minimum Wage cases, in which Frankfurter and others close to Brandeis had some connection. Murphy questioned Brandeis's participation in some war-related cases in 1919 and the Lever Act cases in 1921 because of his advisory activities in the Wilson administration (*Brandeis/Frankfurter Connection*, 54-55). Those cases were, however, less clear than *Stewart Machine Co. v. Davis*. Also less clear was Brandeis's participation in *United States v. Butler*, 297 U.S. 1 (1936). Gardner Jackson said in his oral-history memoir at Columbia University that he, Jerome Frank, Tom Blaisdell, and Lee Pressman met with Brandeis at his home in Chatham in the summer of 1934 to have "a heart-to-heart, off-the-record talk with Brandeis." Jackson recalled that the discussion "dealt with the legality of the Triple-A Act," which would be the crucial issue in *Butler*. "I can remember," said Jackson, "just as a matter of impression, that upon our departure from the powwow with him [Brandeis], Jerome and Tommy Blaisdell both felt very much encouraged that we would not be knocked out in whatever was going on in the Triple-A., if Brandeis's attitudes were to prevail, which subsequent events proved to be a wrong interpretation actually." Jackson's memoir is of questionable reliability because of internal inconsistencies and errors. Brandeis may have given his opinion on the constitutionality of the Triple-A before he sat in judgment on that issue in *Butler*, but more evidence than Jackson's memoir is needed to prove it. *Butler* has been cited by both Murphy (*Brandeis/Frankfurter Connection*, 142) and Strum (*Brandeis*, 403) as illustrating Brandeis's ability to vote on the basis of legal principle despite the fact he had expressed a personal opinion to the contrary. Strum may have had *Butler* in mind when she wrote that "Brandeis seems to have been both unethical and honest": unethical because of immersion in policy-making as in the unemployment compensation legislation and honest because of his judgment according to legal principles as in *Butler* (ibid., 404). If Pusey is correct, Brandeis wavered in his decision in *Butler*. He had not yet made up his mind when the case was voted in conference and only later recorded his dissenting vote. Even then, his vote apparently was not firm, for when Stone circulated his dissenting opinion in the case, it "almost cost him the vote of Justice Brandeis" (Merlo J. Pusey, *Charles Evans Hughes* [New York: Macmillan, 1951], 744-45).

82. *New York Times*, Feb. 18, 1982, A22.

83. Felix Frankfurter, *Of Law and Men* (New York: Harcourt, Brace & Co., 1956), 188.

84. Paper to Danelski, Dec. 14, 1983.

85. Alfred Lief, *Brandeis: The Personal History of an American Ideal* (New York: Stackpole Sons, 1936), 397.

86. *New York Times*, July 18, 1916, 8.

87. Brandeis to Hugo Pam, July 21, 1916, BL, 4:251.

Brandeis and the New Deal

NELSON L. DAWSON

In late 1932 Louis D. Brandeis was a seventy-six-year-old Supreme Court justice and political activist who was eagerly anticipating a new age of reform. The exhilarating days of Woodrow Wilson's first term, when Brandeis had played a significant role in shaping policy, had been followed by World War I and a decade of Republican control. The Progressive remnant that survived into the twenties was forced to operate under severe constraints.[1] Franklin D. Roosevelt's election, however, brought new hope to all reformers and gave Brandeis a last opportunity to influence national political policy. Brandeis's deeply held social philosophy provided the general guidelines that governed his efforts to shape New Deal policy while an awareness of his own finitude undoubtedly spurred his efforts.[2]

Brandeis's social philosophy can be understood only in the context of his intense moral convictions. While he had little apparent interest in formal theology, he had a deep commitment to an austere Biblical morality; there was good reason for Roosevelt to call him "Isaiah."[3] At times this stance led to unlikely alliances. Concerned over the decadence of the twenties, he once urged William Jennings Bryan, whom he called "the preacher of righteousness," to "wage a crusade for decency and righteousness."[4]

Brandeis had advocated many reforms since his early days as the "People's Attorney," but his varied activities are generally explicable by his denunciation of "the curse of bigness." He believed that enduring reform could only occur if both business and government were reduced to manageable size as had been attempted during Wilson's first term. Brandeis's opposition to bigness drew fire from contemporary critics who accused him of trying to "turn the clock back."[5] Nevertheless, over the years Brandeis's economic views have been accorded a generally sympathetic hearing. His opposition to the trusts, his emphasis on competition, and his concern for small businessmen have placed him firmly in the Progressive tradition. More recently, however, his views have been criticized. Thomas K. McCraw has subjected them to a particularly trenchant analysis.

McCraw asserts that Brandeis never really understood the nature of big business, that he did not distinguish between various kinds of trusts, and that his opposition to bigness was an *idée fixe* that "contributed to the institutionalization of a confused and contradictory regulatory program, one that stood almost no chance of working."[6] McCraw accuses Brandeis of an elitist position that did not favor consumers but rather the small shopkeepers "in their war against large, price-cutting retailers." He opposed large, integrated firms in favor of the inefficient smaller companies as much for political and ideological reasons as for economic reasons. Furthermore, McCraw concludes, his program for decentralization would "likely have required nothing short of authoritarian action by the state."[7]

This is a formidable indictment and one that deserves a more extended analysis than it can receive here. Certainly, Brandeis remained unalterably opposed to bigness as a first principle. Yet he seemed surprisingly flexible on the central question of the relationship between size and efficiency. Brandeis's analysis of business enterprise seems far more pragmatic and sophisticated than McCraw's description would indicate.[8] Economic analysis of this kind is difficult. While McCraw's critique merits careful consideration, the provisional conclusion seems best summed up in the old Scottish verdict "not proven." But whatever the outcome of the current debate over the validity of Brandeis's economic perspective might be, the fact is that this perspective is what provided the framework in which he evaluated specific New Deal policies.

Brandeis was also convinced, however, that enduring reform depends not only on the right policies but also on their implementation by the right people. Personnel is as important as legislation. This belief provided the rationale for Brandeis's intense activity as a New Deal recruiting officer. This persistent, behind-the-scenes effort was not a mere quest for personal power but rather an attempt to implement the policies he believed essential to economic recovery and political reform.[9]

Brandeis confronted the opportunity offered by the New Deal not only with his general and widely known social philosophy but also with a specific recovery program that has received less attention.[10] Brandeis's recovery program was Keynesian in the broad sense and was based on the conviction that massive government spending would stimulate the economy sufficiently to produce recovery. He advocated an ambitious public works program consisting of projects of permanent value, such as soil conservation, afforestation, flood control, and navigational improvements. Since such a program would require enormous government spending at a time when money was scarce, Brandeis advocated rigorous taxation of wealthy individuals and large corporations to raise the necessary revenue.[11] This program was more conservative than John M. Keynes's approach because it sought to avoid deficit spending.[12] While the various elements of this program were not original with Brandeis, he combined them in such a way as to produce a distinctive approach to recovery that he urged persistently throughout the New Deal years.

From Brandeis's perspective this approach had several advantages. Obviously, he believed it would produce recovery. It would, furthermore, do so in a simple and direct manner that was consistent with his general social philosophy. The public works projects would become permanent national assets. Many of them were intended to improve the plight of the nation's farmers, a source of deep concern to Brandeis. By providing jobs for the unemployed, the public works projects would maintain their self-respect as productive citizens as well as contribute to the national welfare. Brandeis's tax reforms reflected his belief in the curse of bigness and the evils of concentrated wealth. It is not surprising, therefore, that Brandeis evaluated New Deal policy in all its bewildering complexity by the simple standard of how it would affect the implementation of his recovery program. This is the key to understanding the promise and the frustration of the New Deal from Brandeis's perspective.

There was a basic conflict within Brandeis's social philosophy that he was never able to resolve. The conflict is inescapable for political activists who oppose a powerful central government. Brandeis had a profound distrust of strong government, and he opposed the early New Deal emphasis on central planning as it was expressed in the National Recovery Administration (NRA) and the Agricultural Adjustment Administration (AAA). Yet his recovery program required a powerful federal government capable of launching a massive public works program financed by heavy taxation of the rich and powerful. Such an approach not only required a strong government but could be expected to increase its power. Brandeis never resolved this conflict, but it is doubtful if he was much troubled by it because, like all pragmatists, he was more interested in results than in consistency. He opposed governmental power in general, but he advocated it, if only indirectly, when it was essential to secure the ends he thought necessary to recovery.

Brandeis confronted the opportunity offered by Roosevelt's election from his position on the Supreme Court, a position he deeply valued and yet one that imposed certain constraints on his political activism.[13] His reluctance to act directly led him to depend on a complex network of personal contacts within administrative circles to provide information and to influence policy decisions. The essential link was the relationship between Brandeis, Felix Frankfurter, and Roosevelt. Frankfurter first encountered Brandeis while a student at the Harvard Law School in May 1905 when he heard Brandeis speak on "The Opportunity of the Law," a speech that discussed the contributions activist lawyers could make to the creation of a better society.[14]

Brandeis and Frankfurter became friends in Washington, D.C., in 1911 during Brandeis's business trips from Boston.

Their friendship deepened despite Frankfurter's support of Theodore Roosevelt during the presidential campaign of 1912 when Brandeis emerged as one of Wilson's most influential advisers. In 1913 Brandeis helped obtain Frankfurter's appointment to the faculty of the Harvard Law School, and by 1916 the letter salutation "Dear Mr. Frankfurter" had become "Dear Felix"; the first-name greeting was a singular honor in Brandeis's circle of acquaintances. In 1919 Brandeis wrote Marion Denman, Frankfurter's fiancée, that he had become "half brother—half son."[15]

Brandeis's growing friendship with Frankfurter occurred at a crucial time in his career because his Supreme Court appointment in 1916 imposed restraints on his political involvements. Frankfurter, therefore, began to act as Brandeis's agent in a variety of social causes, and Brandeis began supplementing Frankfurter's income to subsidize these efforts. From 1926 to 1938, Frankfurter received $3,500 a year, an amount equivalent to over $30,000 in 1988 dollars.[16] With Brandeis's support, Frankfurter became a liberal gadfly. He wrote articles for progressive publications, particularly the *New Republic*, supported reform legislation, defended Sacco and Vanzetti, and labored for Zionism. At the same time, Frankfurter also worked at cultivating a large number of potentially useful people with those skillful techniques of influence—including outright flattery—that he called "personalia."[17] Brandeis had found the ideal representative.

The relationship of Frankfurter and Roosevelt, however, did not develop in such a progressive fashion. Frankfurter and Roosevelt first met at the Harvard Club in New York City in 1906, but there was little contact until World War I when they both served on the War Labor Policies Board.[18] Another gap in their relationship followed and lasted until 1928. Frankfurter later reported, rather unconvincingly, that he had simply "lost sight" of Roosevelt during this ten-year period.[19] It is not surprising that the opportunistic Frankfurter reviewed the relationship in 1928 after Roosevelt had been elected governor of New York. Then he began to offer unsolicited suggestions on both policy and personnel. A closer relationship slowly developed so that Frankfurter later recalled that by

1932 they had formed "rather easy, I might say, intellectually intimate ties."[20] This developing relationship did not remove all of Brandeis's and Frankfurter's reservations regarding Roosevelt as a presidential candidate. They realized, however, that he was the only viable progressive choice, and after his election the Frankfurter connection became a potentially powerful means of projecting Brandeis's influence into the new administration.[21]

Brandeis did not have to rely solely on his link with Roosevelt, however, because the burgeoning of New Deal agencies provided him with an unprecedented opportunity to place suitable people in government service. The recruits were usually Frankfurter's bright, young protégés.[22] Brandeis constantly sought to increase his influence, casting his nets widely by means of his famous Sunday afternoon teas at his modest apartment. The rooms were stifling in summer. Food was a secondary consideration. But the teas gave Brandeis an opportunity to make contacts, hunt for talent, give advice, and gather information.[23]

Although Brandeis was not involved in Roosevelt's presidential campaign, he nevertheless became an unwelcome figure among some of his advisers. His chief opponent was Rexford Tugwell. Tugwell, A.A. Berle, Jr., and Raymond Moley composed a group of academic advisers called the Brain Trust that was committed to central planning. They were convinced that the government planning agencies of World War I were the relevant models for dealing with the depression. The Brains Trusters, particularly Tugwell, opposed what they regarded as Brandeis's outmoded perspective. They ignored his recovery program and argued that his opposition to bigness was Jeffersonian nostalgia for a simpler America.[24]

The difference of opinion was aggravated by suspicion. As early as the fall of 1932, Tugwell was complaining about Brandeis's "mysterious channels" of influence that he described in conspiratorial terms. He did not, however, criticize Brandeis's activities as violations of judicial propriety.[25] Berle's opposition to Brandeis's philosophy was increased by his dislike of Frankfurter, who had been one of his professors and with whom he had clashed while a student at the Harvard

Law School.[26] Brandeis had a better relationship with Moley than with any of the other Brains Trusters. He thought that Moley was more receptive to his opinions and sought to transmit the details of his recovery program to Roosevelt through him by way of Frankfurter. Moley may have been more receptive than his colleagues, but he never really accepted Brandeis's program despite receiving the full Frankfurter treatment—over 150 letters from January to September 1933. In any case, his usefulness to Brandeis diminished in 1934 as he drifted away from Roosevelt.[27]

Roosevelt created a minor crisis for Brandeis at the beginning of his administration by offering to appoint Frankfurter solicitor-general. Frankfurter declined as tactfully as possible by telling Roosevelt that it would be impossible to accept the position and still "have anything to do on any matters on which you might want my help." This response had Brandeis's hearty approval. Roosevelt may have been mildly irritated at the refusal, but there was no significant strain in the relationship. At Brandeis's urging, Frankfurter continued to bombard Roosevelt and his advisers with suggestions on policy and personnel.[28]

The concept of two New Deals involves an oversimplification of the complex legislative record of Roosevelt's first term that has produced historiographical debate.[29] Yet for all of its limitations, it remains a useful way to schematize the first term.[30] The conventional view is that the first New Deal of 1933 featured the central planning of NRA and AAA while the second New Deal of 1935 focused on "Brandeisian" reforms. Another conventional interpretation is that Brandeis opposed the first New Deal and supported the second New Deal, but this position represents another oversimplification.[31] In fact, he was not totally opposed to the first or completely satisfied with the second.

Brandeis did oppose the most important initiatives of the first New Deal, the National Recovery Administration (NRA) and the Agricultural Adjustment Administration (AAA). He had almost no contact with NRA head Hugh Johnson, and he made little effort to place any recruits in the agency. As early as August 1933, Brandeis commented that NRA was

having "troubles galore," implying that it was retarding recovery. The NRA's only possible contribution, Brandeis argued, would be to protect labor organizations and encourage
regularity of employment. By 1934 it was clear that the NRA
was floundering. Eventually, Brandeis voted with a unani-
mous Court to overturn it in the case of *Schechter* v. *United
States* on May 27, 1935.[32]

Brandeis had a long-standing interest in agriculture. His
correspondence with his brother Alfred reveals his concern
over the agricultural depression of the twenties.[33] He was
convinced, however, that the AAA was taking the wrong
approach by aiding the wealthier farmers at the expense of
the agricultural underclass of small farmers, sharecroppers,
and tenants. Even before the agency had begun to function,
Brandeis confided to Frankfurter that he was concerned about
the sweeping production controls that he feared would ac-
centuate the curse of bigness in agriculture. He did not think
that the AAA was unconstitutional, and so he dissented from
the decision in *United States* v. *Butler* (1936) that eventually
overturned it.[34]

Despite their opposition to AAA policy, Brandeis and
Frankfurter were able to place a coterie of reformers in its
legal department. The group was headed by Jerome Frank
and included such bright, young activist lawyers as Nathan
Witt, Lee Pressman, and Alger Hiss. These men and their
allies disrupted AAA policy by the zeal with which they
sought direct assistance for sharecroppers and tenants. Brandeis had supported the Southern Tenant Farmers' Union
(STFU) and had given money to Commonwealth College,
which espoused its positions. In early 1935 AAA head Chester
Davis, angered by the reformers' adoption of positions taken
by the STFU, decided on a purge. Secretary of Agriculture
Henry Wallace reluctantly agreed; Brandeis's tenuous influence in the AAA disappeared. With characteristic under-
statement he observed that "AAA developments are very
regrettable."[35] The purge was a setback but hardly a catas-
trophe since there had been little chance that the activists
could have significantly influenced AAA policy.

Despite disappointment concerning the main thrust of the

first New Deal, Brandeis could take modest satisfaction in some legislation such as the Securities Act of 1933. Secretary of Commerce Daniel Roper asked banker Huston Thompson to work on securities legislation. After an early draft of Thompson's bill ran into trouble in Congress, Moley asked Frankfurter to work on another draft. Thompson had asked Brandeis for advice, but Brandeis's interest was focused on Frankfurter's effort. So he consulted with Frankfurter as well as with James Landis and Benjamin V. Cohen whom Frankfurter had enlisted in the project. In the ensuing competition of drafts, Frankfurter's version won out, much to Brandeis's satisfaction. The measure passed Congress on May 27, 1933.[36]

The establishment of the Tennessee Valley Authority (TVA) was another reason for satisfaction because it was to implement conservation measures that Brandeis had long advocated. The long-standing interest of Sen. George Norris and Roosevelt himself made lobbying by Brandeis unnecessary. Willard Hurst, one of Brandeis's law clerks, recalled that he hailed the TVA as "a great achievement in human inventiveness and regional decentralization." He worked for the placement of David Lilienthal, a Frankfurter protégé, on the TVA's board of directors. Lilienthal battled for Brandeis's "grassroots" conservation policies against the pro-industry stance of the other directors.[37]

Such achievements as TVA and securities legislation, however, were not sufficient to redeem the first New Deal for Brandeis. He remained unreconciled to its planning emphasis. His own recovery program, which he urged incessantly, either directly or through Frankfurter and others, was nowhere close to adoption. This was bad enough, but the situation deteriorated even more as Roosevelt vacillated from late 1933 to the spring of 1935. Apparently puzzled by the failure of the economy to rebound, Roosevelt tried Brandeis's patience with his flounderings. In some desperation, Roosevelt clutched at the monetary theory of George Warren who believed that a reduction in the gold value of the dollar would raise prices and promote recovery. In August he began a gold-buying policy that alarmed Brandeis. Although Roosevelt soon abandoned the futile policy, Brandeis remained disillusioned. By unhappy coincidence, Frankfurter was in England during this crucial period from September 1933 to August 1934. So Brandeis was without Frankfurter's help during the worst phase of Roosevelt's indecisiveness. Their correspondence during this period is pervaded with deep pessimism.[38]

In Frankfurter's absence, Brandeis turned to several of his protégés for help, particularly to Benjamin Cohen, Thomas Corcoran, and James Landis who worked on the Securities Exchange Act, one of the few significant measures passed in 1934 and one that established the Securities Exchange Commission. Although Brandeis approved of the regulatory power granted to the new commission, such measures were peripheral. His recovery program was nowhere close to adoption. From England Frankfurter continued to shower Roosevelt with advice without apparent effect.[39]

Brandeis was anxious for Frankfurter to return quickly and plunge immediately into action. Brandeis was troubled by the possibility that Roosevelt's first term would end in failure. Upon his return, Frankfurter, always the point man for Brandeis's initiatives, was intensively reoriented by conferences with Brandeis himself along with Cohen, Corcoran, and others. With Brandeis urging him on, Frankfurter saw Roosevelt several times in the summer and fall of 1934 to exhort him to regain the initiative by adopting Brandeis's recovery program.[40]

Roosevelt eventually responded to the encouragement of Frankfurter and other discontented liberals. The result was the second New Deal. He announced a new program in his January 1935 message to Congress, but he did not present it in detail until the following spring. Brandeis responded to this opportunity with redoubled efforts to influence policy and to place protégés in key positions. After considerable effort, Frankfurter succeeded in having Corcoran, one of his most trusted lieutenants, named a special assistant to the president. This appointment in March 1935 raised Brandeis's hopes for the eventual adoption of his recovery program.[41]

One of Brandeis's long-standing concerns was regularity of employment; he had been grappling with the issue for years, and eventually it emerged from behind-the-scenes con-

sideration in time to be included in the legislative program of
the second New Deal. In accordance with his general social
philosophy, Brandeis advocated a decentralized program on
the state level in which employees placed part of their wages
in a trust fund in amounts proportionate to the average annual
employment rate for their particular industry. This reserve
fund would then be kept by the employers in times of full
employment.[42]

Brandeis's daughter Elizabeth Raushenbush and her husband Paul, both professors at the University of Wisconsin,
lobbied successfully for the Wisconsin legislature to pass a
law that embodied Brandeis's approach in early 1932. This
so-called Wisconsin Plan was, however, challenged by a centralized alternative advocated by Abraham Epstein, called the
Ohio Plan. The Ohio Plan stipulated a centrally pooled fund.
Its basic goals were unemployment and old age insurance
rather than regularity of employment. An intense debate developed over the merits of the rival plans.[43]

Brandeis urged others to support the Wisconsin Plan, and
he also lobbied vigorously for it behind the scenes.[44] Yet the
final result was disappointing. The original draft of the social
security law, called the Wagner-Lewis Bill, was strongly Brandeisian, but subsequent compromises, which Roosevelt accepted, greatly weakened it. By March 1935 Brandeis was
deeply pessimistic, commenting to Frankfurter that any measure passed during the rest of the year would be "unutterably
bad." When the Social Security Act passed Congress in August 1935, Brandeis and Frankfurter maintained a disap-
pointed silence.[45]

Brandeis was deeply interested in tax policy because his
recovery program was dependent on increased revenue. Despite the politically sensitive nature of the issue, there were
some hopeful signs by late 1934 when Roosevelt instructed
Secretary of the Treasury Henry Morgenthau to consult with
Frankfurter on the matter. The two men were rivals, so Morgenthau must have been chagrined while Frankfurter expressed amusement at his discomfiture.[46] In December 1934
the Treasury Department unveiled a major tax reform program that included such Brandeisian features as increases in

gift and inheritance taxes along with corporate taxes. At this crucial point, however, Roosevelt hesitated, creating widespread disillusionment among liberals. Brandeis and Frankfurter were alarmed at Roosevelt's vacillation, and Frankfurter helped arrange a conference between Roosevelt and key congressional liberals in May 1935.[47]

This liberal pressure along with Roosevelt's growing concern over the popularity of such potential rivals as Huey Long helped restimulate his progressive zeal. Frankfurter helped maintain this momentum by spending much time in the White House during the summer of 1935 where he enjoyed regular access to Roosevelt. Roosevelt sent Congress a strong tax bill that contained the Treasury Department recommendations. Congress, however, reacted to powerful opposition by significantly weakening the bill before passing it in late August. Brandeis tried to stay optimistic by claiming that Roosevelt had "come out on top," but he knew better.[48]

In July 1934 the National Power Policy Committee had been created to deal with the complex problems posed by the public utility holding companies. The issue was one of great importance to Brandeis who had long been concerned about the curse of bigness as it existed in the power industry. He was particularly hopeful when Benjamin Cohen was named general counsel for the committee and began drafting legislation.[49]

A strange impasse occurred. Cohen advocated strict regulation of the holding companies rather than outright abolition. Brandeis also favored this approach because he believed that a rigid law mandating abolition would prove unenforceable as had happened with the Sherman Antitrust Act of 1890. Roosevelt, however, favored abolition. In August Frankfurter, who was still in the White House much of the time, hammered out a compromise that eliminated the "death sentence" provision and enabled the measure to pass. The Public Utility Holding Company Act represented a kind of victory even though the final form had been weakened and enforcement in the future proved ineffective.[50]

The question of public works was of concern to Brandeis because of its implications for his recovery program. In fact,

Frankfurter had consistently urged Roosevelt to support a massive public works commitment of up to $5 billion a year ever since his return from England. Despite these efforts, however, the Emergency Relief Appropriation Act that passed Congress in April 1935 fell considerably below what Brandeis had hoped for. Frankfurter congratulated Roosevelt on the passage of the act, but his remarks were perfunctory.[51]

The second New Deal was not a great triumph for the Brandeisian social philosophy. The public works and tax measures were too weak to be of any significance in implementing his recovery program. The social security and holding company legislation was desirable but flawed; neither focused on recovery. Brandeis, in fact, showed little interest in some of what are regarded as the most significant accomplishments of the second New Deal. He had little to say about relief despite his approval of its humanitarianism because he did not think it promoted recovery. He also showed little interest in Robert Wagner's National Labor Relations Act or, indeed, in labor issues generally.[52]

From Brandeis's perspective, in fact, the second New Deal was at best only a mild success. He could feel optimism only because he hoped that such modest achievements would prove to be the foundation of a new offensive that would continue until his long-term goals could be attained. For a time this seemed likely, particularly after Roosevelt's landslide victory in 1936. In retrospect, however, it is clear that by this time the New Deal was losing momentum. So without Brandeis realizing it, his last chance for substantive progress was slipping away. Roosevelt's disastrous effort to change the composition of the Supreme Court in 1937 was both a cause and a symptom of this situation.

Roosevelt had been concerned about the reaction of the Supreme Court to reform legislation since the beginning of the New Deal. The so-called Black Monday decisions in May 1935 gave dramatic expression to the tension between the Court and the New Deal. It is true that the three decisions did not significantly alter the course of the administration. Only the case of *Schechter* v. *United States*, which overturned the NRA, involved basic policy. Nevertheless, Roosevelt took

the decisions badly and struck back by denouncing the Court
for embracing a "horse and buggy" view of the Constitution.
The Court went on to overturn the AAA in 1936.[53] It is true
that the NRA and AAA had proved to be ineffective, but
Roosevelt reacted vigorously because he could only assume
that the Court would continue its pattern of rejecting New
Deal legislation. In the euphoria of his tremendous victory in
1936, he decided to strike back. Unfortunately, the method
he chose ultimately damaged his prestige and strained his
relationship with Brandeis.[54]

In January 1937 Roosevelt warned Frankfurter of an im-
pending "awful shock" and asked him to suspend judgment
until they could confer. The "awful shock" was a court reform
bill that would enable the president to appoint new federal
judges for all those who did not retire at the age of seventy.
Although all federal courts were included, the obvious target
was the recalcitrant Supreme Court. Roosevelt consulted with
very few advisers regarding this bill, relying heavily on the
advice of Homer Cummings. Cummings, ironically, got the
idea from the arch-conservative Justice James McReynolds
who had made a similar proposal when he was Wilson's attorney general in 1913.[55]

Brandeis strongly opposed the bill; he told Corcoran, who
first told him of it, that he was "unalterably opposed." Roosevelt, he observed, "was making a great mistake." He was
undoubtedly stung by the implication that he and his older
colleagues were not carrying their share of the Court's work
load, but his objections went far deeper. He could not approve
of what he regarded as a clumsy maneuver to augment presidential power in an arbitrary way. And there was another
factor to be considered. Although Brandeis had always been
one of the Court's liberal mavericks, he was nonetheless a
member of the Court and therefore saw it as only eight other
men were able to. Brandeis had a deeply conservative instinct,
particularly where the Court was concerned, and the Court
bill stimulated it powerfully.[56]

While there was never any doubt about Brandeis's reaction,
Frankfurter's position was ambiguous. His published work
on judicial matters indicated a philosophical opposition to

such schemes as the Court bill. However, his relationship with Roosevelt, which by 1937 had become the basis of a possible Supreme Court appointment, ensured that a break with Roosevelt on this issue would be a wrenching experience. So Frankfurter apparently tried to convince himself that the bill was justified. His attempts to defend it, however, seem halfhearted and querulous; they were not up to his usual standard of spirited rhetoric.[57] Already hard-pressed on the issue, Frankfurter's position was made even more difficult by Brandeis's flagrant opposition. Brandeis was instrumental in bringing together two of the bill's key opponents—Chief Justice Charles Evans Hughes and Burton K. Wheeler, chairman of the Senate Judiciary Committee. Their meeting led to Hughes's letter to the committee that effectively refuted Roosevelt's rationale for the proposal.[58]

Frankfurter reacted to Brandeis's activities with deep disapproval. In late March he wrote him an anguished letter, never sent, in which he expressed resentment at "the C. J. [Hughes] putting you on the front line even with your approval." Several days later he wrote Brandeis to denounce Hughes's letter as an unwarranted intervention in a political matter; he concluded, "I am sorry to write thus, but I am very, very sad." Brandeis replied laconically, "I reserve comment on what you say until there is chance for talk, saying only that you are laboring under some misapprehensions." They met in April and agreed not to discuss the matter in order to avoid any further strain on their relationship.[59]

What is the significance of the struggle over Roosevelt's Court bill? It certainly resulted in a bitter personal defeat for the president even though it undoubtedly contributed to the Court's liberal shift beginning in 1937. In retrospect, however, it seems doubtful if it altered the course of the New Deal in any major way. The defeat revealed the strength of an emerging conservative coalition. The Court struggle probably accelerated the combination of opposition forces, but clearly the loss of the momentum for reform would have occurred in any case. The struggle, furthermore, did not permanently affect the Brandeis-Frankfurter-Roosevelt connection. All relationships were eventually restored though they were perhaps never quite the same, particularly the relationship between Brandeis and Roosevelt.[60] The Brandeis-Frankfurter relationship was certainly changing, but the Court struggle was not the underlying cause. In 1937 Brandeis was eighty-one years old, only two years from retirement while Frankfurter was fifty-six years old, only two years from a Supreme Court appointment. Their relationship had slowly begun to reflect Frankfurter's increased responsibilities over the years. By the mid-thirties, their relationship had become collegial.

But in any case whatever residual strains might have been left over from the Court struggle, they could not have affected Brandeis's impact on the New Deal simply because by the late thirties the New Deal had lost its momentum and there were few legislative initiatives even in the face of the ongoing economic crisis. The correspondence of Brandeis and Frankfurter reflects this situation. Their letters reveal a shift from participation to observation. There was a growing sense of puzzlement and detachment. Brandeis and Frankfurter had strongly criticized Roosevelt during his vacillations of 1934, but they were silent during the floundering of 1938. Even reformers as sanguine as Brandeis and Frankfurter confessed to an uncharacteristic bewilderment. "It's all strangely obscure—why things go down so disastrously & why they gradually seem to be climbing up." Brandeis, for his part, welcomed the economic upswing but confessed that he could see "nothing which suggests a solution of our problems."[61]

In 1938 Brandeis was compelled to face both the limitations of the New Deal and the constraints of declining health. He confronted the latter with his characteristic realism and dignity as he resigned from the Court in March 1939. Frankfurter, who had clearly attained his full professional maturity, was appointed to the Court later in the year.[62] So the New Deal partnership ended at last with Brandeis in retirement and Frankfurter on the Court during a vastly different era of global conflict in which domestic concerns declined in urgency. One of the New Deal's most significant partnerships ended along with the New Deal itself as Dr. Win the War replaced Dr.

New Deal. Brandeis continued his intense interest in public affairs and came to appreciate Roosevelt's rising stature as a leader of the beleaguered democracies. Yet he also continued to chafe at the unwelcome inactivity. In May 1940 he confided sadly to his niece, "All I can do now is let people talk to me and imagine I help them, but I don't."[63]

Brandeis's lifelong commitment to political activism ensured that he was a perennially controversial figure from his early days as the "People's Attorney" through the turbulent battle for confirmation to the Supreme Court to his later career as a progressive justice on a conservative Court. It would probably be a source of wry amusement for him to know that he remains a controversial figure over forty years after his death. Various aspects of Brandeis's career have generated scholarly debate over the years, but it is the issue of judicial propriety that has most recently put him once again before the public eye.[64] It is clear that Brandeis never manifested that Olympian detachment from political matters expected of Supreme Court justices. His activities, furthermore, intensified during the opportunity afforded by the New Deal. He certainly violated the recognized canons of judicial propriety. Indeed, it is arguable that the intensity and duration of his political activity while on the Court is unparalleled.[65] Furthermore, Brandeis was aware of the impropriety because he was careful to conceal his activities and maintain the appearance of detachment.[66]

Yet it seems clear that Brandeis did not act unethically; one can argue that he did so only by uncritically identifying unethical behavior with impropriety. Brandeis acted selflessly, and he held his protégés to the same high standards that governed his own behavior. He was not interested in power, prestige, or money. To regard him as a Machiavellian conspirator is to do him a great injustice. This debate over Brandeis's political activities might well have sounded somewhat strange to him. It is certainly possible that, however much deference he felt was necessary to disarm contemporary opinion, he did not think of his activities as political in character. While it is impossible to reconstruct his own thoughts on this issue, it is clear that he was not interested in partisan issues as such. He was undoubtedly convinced that he was doing the right things for the right reasons for the public good during a time of great national emergency.

We are not, to be sure, excused merely by the sincerity of our rationalizations, and this is a potentially dangerous one. There are many people eager to justify misbehavior by appealing to the public good while acting in an ostensibly disinterested manner. Some of the great tyrants of history have done this. But, as Frankfurter once observed, "everything turns on men."[67] There is Cicero and there is Cataline; there is Huey Long and there is Louis D. Brandeis. His behavior can ultimately be judged not only by his methods but also by his intentions and by his results.

In the last analysis, there is an ironic sense in which this debate seems curiously inconsequential because of the limitations Brandeis encountered in seeking to influence the New Deal. At first there was reason for optimism. His early efforts during Wilson's first term had been largely successful. Then after the barren years of the twenties, Brandeis, near the end of his career, was buoyed by the promise of the New Deal. It is not surprising, given the circumstances, that he was not inclined to be inhibited by canons of judicial propriety. Yet the promise of the New Deal turned to frustration; for all his efforts Brandeis could not shape the New Deal as he wished.

It might have been some consolation for him to reflect that no one else could either. In a very real sense, Brandeis was defeated by his perennial nemesis—the curse of bigness. The New Deal was a pivotal event in administrative size and complexity. So while there are many secondary explanations for Brandeis's frustration, the primary reason may well be simply that no one, including Roosevelt himself, could control that booming, buzzing confusion called the New Deal. Brandeis's frustration was prophetic. Must a government big enough to grapple with the increasingly complex problems of modern society also become too big to function effectively? Is the curse of bigness ineluctable? We have inherited this perplexing question from the era of Brandeis and the New Deal. It raises an issue of perennial relevance for the America of the twentieth and twenty-first centuries.

---

1. For discussions of Brandeis and Wilson's New Freedom, see Alpheus T. Mason, *Brandeis: A Free Man's Life* (New York: Viking Press, 1946), 375-441; Lewis J. Paper, *Brandeis* (Englewood Cliffs, N.J.: Prentice-Hall, 1983), 167-81; Philippa Strum, *Louis D. Brandeis: Justice for the People* (Cambridge, Mass.: Harvard Univ. Press, 1984), 196-223; Melvin I. Urofsky, "Wilson, Brandeis, and the Trust Issue, 1912-1914," *Mid-America* 49 (1967): 3-28.

2. The secondary literature on Brandeis's thought is voluminous. See the standard biographies by Mason, Paper, and Strum and their bibliographies. The best introduction, however, is provided by Brandeis's own works. See especially *Business—A Profession* (Boston: Small, Maynard, 1914); *Other People's Money—and How the Bankers Use It* (New York: Frederick A. Stokes, 1914); and *The Curse of Bigness and Miscellaneous Papers* (New York: Viking Press, 1934). A good overview is provided by Melvin I. Urofsky in *A Mind of One Piece: Brandeis and American Reform* (New York: Charles Scribner's Sons, 1971).

3. David Riesman to Frankfurter, May 22, 1936, Felix Frankfurter Papers, Library of Congress, Box 24 (abbreviated hereafter as FP); Urofsky, *Mind of One Piece*, 98. For Roosevelt's description of Brandeis as "Isaiah," see Arthur M. Schlesinger, Jr., *The Politics of Upheaval* (Boston: Houghton Mifflin, 1960), 222.

4. Ruth Bryan to Brandeis, Aug. 10, 1933, Louis D. Brandeis Papers, University of Louisville Archives, Supreme Court file (SC) 13, folder 1 (abbreviated hereafter as BP).

5. See, for example, A.A. Berle, Jr., and Gardiner Means, *The Modern Corporation and Private Property* (New York: Macmillan, 1933), viii. Rexford Tugwell was another particularly vigorous contemporary critic.

6. Thomas K. McCraw, "Brandeis and the Origins of the FTC," in *Prophets of Regulation* (Cambridge, Mass.: Harvard Univ. Press, 1984), 94, 99-101. Quote on 94.

7. Ibid., 105-9. See also Thomas K. McCraw, "Louis D. Brandeis Reappraised," *American Scholar*, Autumn 1985, 525-36. L.J. Davis presents a more popularly written analysis in "Other People's Money," *Harper's*, Feb. 1984, 62-64.

8. Brandeis, for example, realized that the relationship of size to efficiency was complex by commenting at one point: "A large part

of our people have also learned that efficiency in business does not grow indefinitely with the size of the business. Very often a business grows in efficiency as it grows from a small business to a large business. . . . a business may be too large to be efficient as well as too small." See Brandeis, *Curse of Bigness*, 109.

9. For an overview of Brandeis's recruiting activities, see Nelson L. Dawson, *Louis D. Brandeis, Felix Frankfurter, and the New Deal* (Hamden, Conn.: Archon Books, 1980), 47-60.

10. Brandeis's recovery program has been generally ignored by historians of the period, and his response to the New Deal has been evaluated almost entirely in terms of his general social philosophy. The result has been not a distorted picture but certainly an incomplete one. See Dawson, *Brandeis, Frankfurter, and the New Deal*, 173-76.

11. Brandeis did not present his recovery program systematically or publicly, possibly out of a desire to avoid openly identifying himself with specific proposals. This is clearly different from identification with his broad social philosophy that was already known long before he became a member of the Supreme Court. Researchers must depend on brief expositions of his recovery program scattered in his correspondence and in the reminiscences of those he discussed it with. See, for example, Journal of David E. Lilienthal, June 3, 1933, David E. Lilienthal Papers, Princeton University; Brandeis to Frankfurter, Jan. 31, 1933, FP, Box 28. For Brandeis's evaluation of Keynes, see Dawson, *Brandeis, Frankfurter, and the New Deal*, 32-33.

12. Brandeis's preference for this approach was undoubtedly due to his legendary frugality and austere life-style as well as to his general economic conservatism. See, for example, Strum, *Brandeis*, 47-49.

13. The issue of Brandeis and judicial propriety during the New Deal has generated much recent debate. See above, pp. 54-55.

14. Livia Baker, *Felix Frankfurter* (New York: Coward-McCann, 1969), 17.

15. Brandeis to Marion Denman, Nov. 3, 1919, FP, Box 28. Brandeis had a beloved brother, Alfred, who died in 1928 but no sons. For an overview of the developing relationship between Brandeis, Frankfurter, and Roosevelt, see Nelson L. Dawson, "Louis D. Brandeis, Felix Frankfurter, and Franklin D. Roosevelt: The Origins of a New Deal Relationship," *American Jewish History* 68 (1978): 32-42.

16. Dawson, *Brandeis, Frankfurter, and the New Deal*, 1-6. See also Bruce Allen Murphy, *The Brandeis/Frankfurter Connection: The Secret*

Political Activities of Two Supreme Court Justices (New York: Oxford Univ. Press, 1982), 35-45.

17. Dawson, *Brandeis, Frankfurter, and the New Deal*, 3-10. See H.N. Hirsch, *The Engima of Felix Frankfurter* (New York: Basic Books, 1981) for a provocative analysis of Frankfurter's personality that deals with his great persuasive and manipulative powers. For a more detailed account of the Brandeis-Frankfurter collaboration before the New Deal, see David W. Levy and Bruce Allen Murphy, "Preserving the Progressive Spirit in a Conservative Time: The Joint Reform Efforts of Justice Brandeis and Professor Felix Frankfurter, 1916-1933," *Michigan Law Review* 78 (1980): 1252-1304.

18. Dawson, "Origins," 38-39.

19. Harlan B. Phillips, ed., *Felix Frankfurter Reminisces* (New York: Reynal, 1960), 236.

20. Ibid., 239; Dawson, "Origins," 40; idem, *Brandeis, Frankfurter, and the New Deal*, 6-10. Frankfurter is probably overstating the case at this point.

21. Frankfurter was particularly vigorous in his reservations, criticizing Roosevelt's relations with Tammany Hall and assuring Al Smith of his support; even his occasional expressions of confidence in Roosevelt seemed halfhearted and unconvincing. See Frankfurter to Walter Notestein, Dec. 17, 1931, FP, Box 86; Frankfurter to Samuel E. Morison, June 9, 1932, FP, Box 85; Frankfurter to Hans Zinsser, Nov. 1, 1932, FP, Box 114.

22. Dawson, *Brandeis, Frankfurter, and the New Deal*, 47-60; Murphy, *Brandeis/Frankfurter Connection*, 113-23. References to Frankfurter's recruiting activities are voluminous both in secondary literature and in contemporary accounts. Such ventures were an open secret. For example, Thomas C. Wallen, writing in the conservative *Literary Digest*, mentions Frankfurter's "close contacts with his former students" and comments in neutral terms on his recruitment of James Landis and Thomas G. Corcoran. See his article "The Supreme Court—Nine Mortal Men," *Literary Digest*, April 7, 1934, 46. Frankfurter was attacked in the fifties as a left-wing conspirator and influence peddler by the *American Mercury*, which had by then become an ultraconservative publication. See, for example, Harold L. Varney, "Frankfurter: Man behind the Scenes," *American Mercury*, May 1957, 113-18.

23. Murphy, *Brandeis/Frankfurter Connection*, 120-23. Murphy writes of Brandeis "indoctrinating his proteges and allies" (120). See also Strum, *Brandeis*, 162-63; and Mason, *Brandeis*, 603-4. Brandeis, however, did not recruit along strict ideological lines, but rather

sought bright, capable people who were in general agreement with his outlook. He was interested in competence and commitment to reform rather than in blind obedience.

24. Dawson, *Brandeis, Frankfurter, and the New Deal*, 37-42.

25. Rexford Tugwell, "Notes for a New Deal Diary," p. 13, Rexford Tugwell Papers, FDR Library; Rexford Tugwell, *The Brains Trust* (New York: Doubleday, 1957), 462.

26. A.A. Berle, Jr., "Reminiscences," Columbia Oral History Collection, 22-23; Frankfurter to Max Lerner, March 20, 1953, FP, Box 76.

27. Dawson, *Brandeis, Frankfurter, and the New Deal*, 39-40; Murphy, *Brandeis/Frankfurter Connection*, 106-12. For general background, see Elliot A. Rosen, *Hoover, Roosevelt, and the Brains Trust: From Depression to New Deal* (New York: Columbia Univ. Press, 1977).

28. Frankfurter, Memorandum about the solicitor generalship, March 15, 1933, FP, Box 97; Frankfurter to Roosevelt, March 14, 1933, FP, Box 97. A contributing factor may have been the decidedly cool relationship between Frankfurter and Homer Cummings, Roosevelt's attorney general. The dominating factor, however, was the high visibility and time-consuming duties of a post that would have limited his political activities on Brandeis's behalf.

29. William Wilson, "The Two New Deals: A Valid Historical Concept?" *Historian* 28 (1966): 268-88.

30. Despite the oversimplifications involved, the concept has become so established in the literature that it seems more feasible to use it with prudent regard for its limitations than to abandon it altogether. Certainly, nothing of the scope of the NRA-AAA planning initiative was attempted in the second New Deal. Roosevelt's first term was divided into two bursts of legislation separated by the lull of 1934. So there were two "New Deals" even if there is no completely satisfactory policy differentiation possible.

31. See the essay "Brandeis's Recovery Program and the Historians," in Dawson, *Brandeis, Frankfurter, and the New Deal*, 73-76.

32. Brandeis to Frankfurter, Aug. 14, 1933; Feb. 21, 27, 1934, FP, Box 28; *Schechter* v. *United States*, 295 U.S. 495 (1935). His decision was clearly based on constitutional grounds rather than on personal opinion.

33. For example, Brandeis to Alfred Brandeis, Nov. 25, 1921; July 22, 1924; June 2, 1927, BP, Miscellaneous file (M), folder 4.

34. Brandeis to Frankfurter, Aug. 1, 1933; Feb. 24, 27, 1935, FP, Box 28; *United States* v. *Butler*, 297 U.S. 1 (1936).

35. Dawson, *Brandeis, Frankfurter, and the New Deal*, 72-79; Mur-

phy, *Brandeis/Frankfurter Connection*, 139-43. Murphy characterizes Brandeis's warnings about the AAA as "vituperative" (143). Brandeis to Frankfurter, Feb. 7, 1935, FP, Box 28; Frankfurter to Brandeis, Feb. 19, March 15, 1934, BP, Government file (G), folder 1.

36. Dawson, *Brandeis, Frankfurter, and the New Deal*, 78-81; Murphy, *Brandeis/Frankfurter Connection*, 133-36. The extent of Brandeis's involvement in the details of the drafting is not certain. The written sources are silent. Murphy, depending primarily on interviews, assumes an intense involvement. See Murphy, *Brandeis/Frankfurter Connection*, 135. Robert Cover, in his spirited defense of Brandeis's judicial propriety during the New Deal, specifically defends him against charges of involvement in legislative drafting. See Robert Cover, "The Framing of Justice Brandeis," *New Republic*, May 5, 1982, 17-18. In a magazine article, Frankfurter credited Brandeis with preparing the climate of opinion for the act by his "impressive analysis of the workings of our financial forces, of the traps and pitfalls that beset the small investor" (Felix Frankfurter, "The Securities Act," *Fortune Magazine*, Aug. 1933, 53-54).

37. Interview of Samuel Konefsky with Willard Hurst, Sept. 14, 1951, quoted in Samuel J. Konefsky, *The Legacy of Holmes and Brandeis: A Study in the Influence of Ideas* (New York: Macmillan, 1956), 173. See also Brandeis to Frankfurter, Feb. 24, June 13, Aug. 3, Aug. 24, 1933, FP, Box 28; and Frankfurter to Roosevelt, June 10, 1933, BP, G 9, folder 2; and Frankfurter to Brandeis, Aug. 12, 1933, FP, Box 28.

38. Brandeis wrote Frankfurter that "FDR seems bent on a policy of monetary stunts which not one economist here . . . believes in & very few even pretend to understand" (Brandeis to Frankfurter, Nov. 17, 1933, BP, G 9, folder 2). See also Frankfurter to Brandeis, Nov. 23, Dec. 9, 18, 1933, BP, G 9, folder 2.

39. Dawson, *Brandeis, Frankfurter, and the New Deal*, 94-100. The evidence indicates that Brandeis advised Cohen, Corcoran, and Landis during the drafting of the Securities Exchange Act. Corcoran reassured Frankfurter during this period that he was keeping in touch with Brandeis (Corcoran to Frankfurter, Nov. 16, Dec. 17, 30, 1933, FP, Boxes 115, 116). See also Murphy, *Brandeis/Frankfurter Connection*, 136-38. Cover argues that Brandeis was not involved directly. See Cover, "Framing," 17-18. Frankfurter to Roosevelt, Feb. 5, 14, May 8, June 8, 1934, FP, boxes 97, 244.

40. Frankfurter to Brandeis, July 20, Aug. 31, 1934, BP, G 9, folder 2; Brandeis to Frankfurter, Aug. 3, 1934, FP, Box 28.

41. Samuel I. Rosenman, ed., *The Public Papers and Addresses of Franklin D. Roosevelt*, 13 vols. (New York: Random House, 1938-50),

4:36; Brandeis to Frankfurter, Oct. 24, 1934, FP, Box 28; Frankfurter to Roosevelt, March 10, 1935, FP, Box 97; Frankfurter to Missy Hand, March 24, 1935, FP, Box 244.

42. Dawson, *Brandeis, Frankfurter, and the New Deal*, 103-12; Murphy, *Brandeis/Frankfurter Connection*, 165-78; "Memo of Mr. Brandeis on Irregular Employment," June 1911, FP, Box 226.

43. Paul A. Raushenbush, "Starting Unemployment Compensation in Wisconsin," *Unemployment Insurance Review* 4 (1967): 17-20; Elizabeth B. Raushenbush, "Wisconsin Tackles Job Security," *Survey*, Dec. 15, 1931, 295-96; Abraham Epstein, "Enemies of Unemployment Insurance," *New Republic*, Sept. 6, 1933, 94-96; Elizabeth B. Raushenbush, "Employment Reserves vs. Insurance," *New Republic*, Sept. 28, 1933, 177-78; Brandeis to Harold Laski, Feb. 28, 1932, BP, M 18, folder 3.

44. Brandeis's correspondence on the subject to Elizabeth, Frankfurter, and others as well as their replies testifies to the intensity of his involvement. See, for example, Brandeis to Elizabeth, Sept. 30, 1933, reprinted in Melvin I. Urofsky and David W. Levy, eds., *The Letters of Louis D. Brandeis*, 5 vols. (Albany, 1971-), 5:523 (abbreviated hereafter as BL); Brandeis to Alice P. Goldmark, Jan. 11, 1934, BL, 5:530-31; Brandeis to Frankfurter, Jan. 10, 1934, FP, Box 28; Elizabeth Raushenbush to Brandeis, Feb. 12, 15, 1934, BP, G 7, folder 1. Frankfurter was also active. See Frankfurter to Brandeis, Feb. 8, 1934; July 18, 20, 26, Aug. 8, 1934, BP, G 9, folder 2; and Frankfurter to Roosevelt, undated (summer 1934), FP, Box 244. Murphy comments that Brandeis's activity on behalf of the Wisconsin Plan constituted "perhaps the most intensive political effort undertaken . . . during this period." See Murphy, *Brandeis/Frankfurter Connection*, 165.

45. Brandeis to Frankfurter, March 25, 1935, FP, Box 28. Frankfurter did not send his customary congratulatory letter to Roosevelt when the measure passed.

46. Brandeis to Frankfurter, May 11, Sept. 29, 1934, FP, Box 28; Frankfurter to Brandeis, Dec. 20, 1934, BP, G 9, folder 2.

47. John M. Blum, ed., *From the Morgenthau Diaries* (Boston: Houghton Mifflin, 1959), 298-300; Raymond Moley, *The First New Deal* (New York: Harcourt, Brace & World, 1966), 531; Brandeis to Frankfurter, Feb. 24, March 12, 1935, FP, Box 28. Frankfurter worked with Boston liberal David K. Niles to arrange a conference. See Niles to Frankfurter, April 22, 1935, quoted in Max Freedman, ed., *Roosevelt and Frankfurter: Their Correspondence, 1928-1945* (Boston: Little, Brown, 1967), 260-61; Roosevelt to Frankfurter, April 20, 1935, FP, Box 98; Frankfurter to Roosevelt, April 30, May 3, May 16, 1935, FP, Box 98.

48. Dean Acheson, *Morning and Noon* (Boston: Houghton Mifflin, 1965), 211; Frankfurter to Brandeis, June 14, July 10, 21, 1935, BP, G 9, folder 2; Sidney Ratner, *American Taxation* (New York: W.W. Norton, 1942), 469-72; *U.S. Statutes at Large*, 49:1014; Brandeis to Frankfurter, Aug. 30, 1935, FP, Box 28.

49. Brandeis, "The Case against the Holding Company," Nov. 23, 1931, Memorandum in the Gifford Pinchot Papers, quoted in Philip J. Funigiello, *Toward a National Power Policy: The New Deal and the Electric Utility Industry* (Pittsburgh: Univ. of Pittsburgh Press, 1973), 21, 42. Funigiello asserts that all opponents of the holding companies "drew from a common intellectual source, Justice Louis D. Brandeis." Frankfurter to Brandeis, Aug. 7, 1932, BP, G 9, folder 2; Frankfurter to Moley, Feb. 28, 1933, FP, Box 28.

50. See Funigiello, *Toward a National Power Policy*, 50-66, 96. The Brandeis-Frankfurter correspondence reflects the ebb and flow of events. See Frankfurter to Brandeis, Dec. 20, 1934; Jan 22, March 15, April 13, June 14, 1935, BP, G 9, folder 2; Brandeis to Frankfurter, March 25, June 20, 1935, FP, Box 28. Neither Brandeis nor Frankfurter commented in writing on the final version of the bill.

51. Frankfurter to Roosevelt, Oct. 16, 25, Nov. 21, 26, 1934; April 29, 1935, FP, Box 97.

52. Dawson, *Brandeis, Frankfurter, and the New Deal*, 122-23. Brandeis never abandoned his support of the preferential shop rather than the closed shop (Brandeis to Frankfurter, Aug. 14, 1933, FP, Box 28).

53. Dawson, *Brandeis, Frankfurter, and the New Deal*, 125-34. Stanley High reported that the NRA decision was "the worst blow the pres. ever had" (Stanley High Diary, March 20, 1936, Stanley High Papers, FDR Library). Roosevelt was also angered by the decision in the case of *Humphrey's Executor* v. *United States*, 295 U.S. 602 (1935). Brandeis wrote the decision in *Louisville Bank* v. *Radford*, 295 U.S. 601 (1935), which overturned the Frazier-Lemke Act. The act was not an administration measure. Brandeis, however, also voted against Roosevelt in the NRA case and the Humphrey case. Harry Hopkins reported that Corcoran and Cohen had told him that Brandeis was "visibly excited and deeply agitated" after the "Black Monday" decisions and that he had told them to tell Roosevelt that "this is the end of this business of centralization." See Harry Hopkins, "Statement to Me by Thomas Corcoran, Giving His Recollection of the Genesis of the Supreme Court Fight," April 3, 1939, Harry Hopkins Papers, FDR Library; Schlesinger, *Politics of Upheaval*, 251. A detailed analysis of Brandeis's decisions in cases involving New Deal legis-

lation would have merit, but the fact is that, paradoxical as it may sound, Brandeis's role as a Supreme Court justice is peripheral to the question of his relation to the New Deal apart from the issue of judicial propriety. It is true that his decisions caused some tensions with Roosevelt, but his judicial integrity was obvious to most unbiased observers. He was willing to uphold the AAA, for example in the case of *United States* v. *Butler* (1936) even though he strongly disapproved of it on political and economic grounds. Brandeis's response to the Court bill caused a much greater crisis than his decisions in the cases involving New Deal legislation.

54. An excellent overview of Roosevelt's Court bill is provided in William Leuchtenburg's "The Origins of Franklin D. Roosevelt's 'Court-Packing' Plan," *Supreme Court Review*, 1966, 347-400.

55. Roosevelt to Frankfurter, Jan. 1, 1937, FP, Box 98; U.S. 75th Cong., 1st Sess., *Senate Reports*, 711; Joseph Alsop and Turner Catledge, *168 Days* (New York, 1938), 31-36.

56. Harry Hopkins, "Memorandum on the Court Fight," quoted in Robert Sherwood, *Roosevelt and Hopkins* (New York: Harper & Brothers, 1948), 90. Hopkins is quoted from a statement Corcoran had made to him. A clue to Brandeis's attitude to the Court can be found in his surprisingly generous estimates of some of his conservative colleagues. See Brandeis to Frankfurter, May 26, 1937; Jan. 5, 1938, FP, Box 28.

57. Frankfurter's response to Roosevelt's letter informing him of the plan was a spirited indictment of the Court's behavior that avoided any discussion of its merits (Frankfurter to Roosevelt, Feb. 7, 1937, FP, Box 98). Among his published writings, see "The Supreme Court and the Public," *Forum*, June 1930, 329-34; and "The Supreme Court of the United States," reprinted in Archibald MacLeish and Edward Prichard, eds., *Law and Politics: Occasional Papers of Felix Frankfurter, 1913-1938* (New York: Capricorn Books, 1962), 21-34. Frankfurter to C.C. Burlingham, March 16, 1937, FP, Box 34.

58. Charles E. Hughes, "Biographical Notes," Charles E. Hughes Papers, Library of Congress, 20-23; interview of A.T. Mason with Burton Wheeler, Feb. 25, 1944, quoted in Mason, *Brandeis*, 626; Joseph Alsop and Turner Catledge, *The 168 Days* (New York: Doubleday, Doran, 1938), 125-26.

59. Frankfurter to Brandeis, March 26, 1937 (unmailed), FP, Box 28; Frankfurter to Brandeis, March 31, 1937, FP, Box 28; Frankfurter to Brandeis, April 5, 1937, FP, Box 28; Brandeis to Frankfurter, April 25, 1937, FP, Box 28; Freedman, *Roosevelt and Frankfurter*, 396.

60. Corcoran was never reconciled to Brandeis as a result of the Court struggle (Cohen to Frankfurter, Oct. 11, 1937, FP, Box 45).

61. Frankfurter to Brandeis, June 24, 1938, BP, SC 22, folder 22; Brandeis to Frankfurter, July 28, 1938, FP, Box 28.

62. Dawson, *Brandeis, Frankfurter, and the New Deal*, 164-67.

63. Fanny Brandeis, Memorandum, May 1940, BP, M 18, folder 1.

64. Much of the debate over Brandeis's political activities and the issue of judicial propriety has been generated by Murphy's *Brandeis/ Frankfurter Connection*. While it is a work of valuable scholarship, Murphy conjures an aura of conspiracy in his interpretation of the Brandeis-Frankfurter relationship and its impact on New Deal policy. A good deal of what Murphy discusses was already known, but he does present a more complete picture than any previously available. The problem is not so much with his facts but with his apparent determination to put the worst possible interpretation on all of Brandeis's activities. For a brief, spirited rebuttal, see Cover, "Framing," 17-21. For a helpful guide to the reviews of Murphy's work, see Gene Teitelbaum, *Justice Louis D. Brandeis: A Bibliography of Writings and Other Materials on the Justice* (Littleton, Colo.: Fred B. Rothman, 1988).

65. Brandeis was by no means the only politically active member of the Supreme Court, though this in itself is no defense. Comparative studies, potentially illuminating, would take us too far afield.

66. Brandeis regularly rejected requests for various extrajudicial activities with the terse notation "precluded." According to Frankfurter, this was one of his favorite words. See Frankfurter to Alexander Bickel, Feb. 4, 1958, FP, Box 127. Hugh Johnson of the NRA caused a minor contretemps in Sept. 1934 when he asserted in a radio talk that he had been in "constant touch" with Brandeis in the early days of the NRA. This was not true, but the concern Brandeis and Frankfurter expressed privately reflects their awareness that other New Deal figures could have made such a statement accurately (Brandeis to Frankfurter, Sept. 14, 22, 23, 1934, FP, Box 28; Frankfurter to Roosevelt, Sept. 20, 1934, FP, Box 97).

67. Frankfurter, "The United States Supreme Court Molding the Constitution," *Current History*, May 1930, 240.

Brandeis, Judaism, and Zionism

ALLON GAL

Louis D. Brandeis represents a classic case of *American* Zionism. (The term *American Zionism* rather than *Zionism in America* is intentional.) A declared Zionist since 1912 and the leader of the Zionist movement in this country from August 1914, Brandeis's conversion to Zionism is intriguing. In 1912 Brandeis was fifty-six years old, a successful lawyer, a nationally recognized Progressive, and a person with a gratifying personal and family life. "What brought Louis Brandeis to Zionism?" is the traditional formulation of the problem by scholars as well as many others. This posing of the question, however, is largely self-defeating. Predating the "Zionization" of Brandeis was the process of his "Judaization." From semiassimilationism Brandeis first moved gradually to acquire Jewish identity and Jewish pride. In a way, his later and famous Zionist "appearance" was a continuation of his growing affirmation of his Jewishness. This positive connection between Judaism and Zionism—a conspicuously American Jewish phenomenon—requires some elaboration.

European Zionism developed a paradoxical, tensional relationship with Judaism. Zionism in Europe came to liberate the Jews from a long, tortured Jewish past; it also came to redeem them from an allegedly docile, submissive, and exilic tradition. On the other hand, European Zionism spoke in the name of an all-embracing Jewish renewal, of a Jewish renaissance.

The dialectical solution of that contradiction was in the

European Zionist concentration on ancient Jewish history, on the epochs of independence. The culture of those sovereign times was often referred to as "Hebrew" rather than as "Jewish." Zionism in Europe, generally speaking, came then to disrupt Jewish continuity, to build a bright, new future while glorifying ancient times.[1]

Zionism in the United States cannot chiefly be accounted for by local rejective or oppressive factors. It did not come to disrupt the inertia of a shameful or distressful history. American Zionism did not have any reason to skip over the immediate American past. Actually, American Jews—Zionists included—tended to take pride in American Jewish history and in the accomplishments of American Jews. (This pride was often expanded to include a nostalgic romanticization of European Jewish history as well.) After all, Jews in America were emancipated without having to raise any real fight for emancipation; and America was for all intents and purposes their home. Zionism in this country thus had the inherent tendency to develop as an extension of the Jewish past. That is, Zionism and Judaism in America had the intrinsic disposition to be mutually interwoven.[2]

Brandeis's concept of Jewish nationalism lacked a clear distinction between Judaism and Zionism. Actually, he tended to blur the two. This happened neither by accident nor as a result of lack of analytical capacity. Rather, this interweaving of Judaism and Zionism expresses, I suggest, the genuine American nature of Brandeis's path to Zionism. Indeed, as we will see later in this chapter, Brandeis's road from semi-assimilation to Zionism decisively testifies to the American qualities of his brand of Jewish nationalism.

Another American aspect of Brandeis's path to Zionism was its nonspeculative nature. Brandeis's changes did not occur as a result of theoretical discussions or ideological revelations. The causes of his transformation were largely rooted in the realities of his life and work as a lawyer, a Progressive, and a Jew.

Louis D. Brandeis spoke on Judaism in public for the first time in November 1905. As a lawyer, his career owed much to Boston Jewry; Brandeis had early and solid business ties with members of his ethnic group. Still, as a Jew, he lived on the margins of that community. As a result of his work as a lawyer and an urban reformer, however, he gradually learned about the potential of the Jewish community on behalf of the causes for which he fought. In the winter of 1905-6, he desperately needed the support of the local community in his crusade to clean up the government of his beloved Boston. He managed to inspire his listeners (Jewish professionals) and to mobilize them while referring to the Torah's ethics and to Jewish ethos in general. As the audience was responsive, Brandeis the Progressive's interest in and appreciation for his ethnic community rose sharply. Earlier teachings of his mother about the moral quality embedded in Judaism and a family tradition about its relatedness to a historic Jewish messianic trend probably served to foster this awakening. When in subsequent years (roughly 1906-9) Brandeis fought for savings bank life insurance and against railroad mergers, he boldly sought—and got—the backing of the Jewish community. His attraction to the Jewish people further deepened in 1910 when he negotiated a compromise in a bitter garment strike that involved Jews on both sides; he sharply sensed then that the same noble ethos was the frame of reference for both employers and workers. The latters' denouncement of injustice in the name of prophetic tradition elated him; thanks to the whole experience he felt belongingness to an eminent Jewish ethical civilization. He was also impressed by the intellectual level of the debates and by the workers' literary versatility. Brandeis's association with Jews also broadened over issues involving the rights of labor, consumers' grievances, and social work. As a consequence of these experiences and contacts, by the end of 1910 Brandeis began to identify publicly and proudly as a Jew.[3]

The next phase in Brandeis's ethnic development—his adoption of Zionism—was a direct continuation of his Judaization. He gradually became a Zionist when he learned that independent Jewish life in Palestine would advance best what he considered sublime in Jewish civilization. What he had found in his American Jewish community, he now discovered, more vigorously expressed, in Jewish Palestine. This process of Brandeis's Zionization was indeed interwoven with his Judaization (and this is one of the reasons why historians find it difficult to ascertain precisely "the date" of Brandeis's Zionist turn). Again, his Zionization was a process, intimately connected with the development of his Jewishness. His gradual adoption of Zionism extended roughly through the years 1909-14. During this phase he was, for example, thrilled to learn about the discovery of the "wild wheat" in Palestine and the possibility that this kind of wheat, sought by botanists for many years, might bring about an agricultural revolution that could eliminate hunger from the world. He found the whole Jewish community in Palestine especially creative and hardworking; and he found there a balance between the enhancement of individual potential and the imperatives of social responsibility. The accomplishments of small, democratic Jewish Palestine were for him a cherished model and an antidote to the stifling monopolization and the oppressive bigness he bitterly fought against in America.[4]

Jewish Palestine was a new hope not merely for Brandeis the Progressive but also for Brandeis the frustated philo-Yankee. He had been a loyal son of New England, steeped in its tradition. The great prominence of Puritan sentiments in Brandeis's personality and philosophy may be traced to his days at Harvard Law School (from 1875). He founded in 1879, together with his best friend, Samuel Warren (an ardent Yankee), a Boston law firm with apparent establishment connections. Actually, the firm never penetrated the big industries of New England nor the financial bastions of Brahmin Boston. Ethnic barriers, however, prevented his acceptance by the group he so identified with. Over a period of many years, Brandeis, as an outsider, came to idealize the Puritan ethos and to internalize it deeply. All this notwithstanding, from about 1905 Brandeis harbored increasing disappointment with the Yankees of his day. He gradually reached the conclusion that they had not properly stood the test of the lofty Puritan heritage. Consequently, he began to see the Zionist endeavor across the ocean as an embodiment of Puritan values. As he changed the focus of his personal identity, Jewish Palestine became for him the early, exemplary New England. In his

eyes the Yishuv (pre-Israel Jewish Palestine) was the restoration of the discredited Puritan world, the true New Zion.[5]

This peculiar Puritan Zionism of Brandeis did reflect, however, the general American circumstances in which his ideology was shaped. Were Brandeis suffering from an
aggressive anti-Semitism, he would not hope for a Jewish
state akin to the "oppressors"; it was because he did *not* encounter anti-Semitism of the European style that Brandeis saw
the Zionist enterprise as a correction of Yankee society. To be
sure, he was maneuvered to "his ethnic place" in social Boston; but this was done quite "gentlemanly." And the subtly
developed pattern did not cause Brandeis and his family any
traumatic experience. True, some Yankee magnates and their
lackeys used anti-Semitism to silence "the radical Jew"; but
this tactic was quite rarely and incidentally employed. Un-
pleasant situations notwithstanding, Brandeis's admiration of
the Yankee's civilization did not dissolve. Moreover, he never
lost hope for bringing America back to its ideals. He trusted
in the American potential for good both domestically and in-
ternationally.

The United States continued to be the home—both physical
and spiritual—for Louis D. Brandeis the Zionist. Beginning
in 1916, he served as a justice of the United States Supreme
Court for twenty-three years. When he died in 1941, he was
buried (to be precise, cremated and buried) in the city in which
he had been born, Louisville, Kentucky. Obviously, his Zionism did not come to supplant his Americanism but rather to
complement it.

Though Brandeis's official leadership of the American
Zionist movement lasted only about two years (August 1914-
July 1916), his influence on American Zionism was tremendous and its impact felt up to his last days. This impact cannot
be accounted for simply as the result of authority derived from
his accomplishments in the society at large; nor can it be fully
explained by his lavish support of Zionist activists and causes.
Undoubtedly, while these factors did help enhance Brandeis's
position, the main source of his influence was a combination
of his powerful personality with a coherent ideology that sensitively reflected the American circumstances.[6]

What were the basic characteristics of Brandeis's Zionism? As is self-evident from his life and career, he did not consider America as "exile." Basically a pluralistic Jeffersonian, he gradually came to conceive the United States as a union of ethnic cultures; in this union the Jewish community could both thrive and work for a better society. Brandeis came to this philosophy, later known as cultural pluralism, through his own experiences and spiritual growth and the influence of the articulate Zionist philosopher, Horace Kallen. In his comprehensive address of April 1915, "The Jewish Problem— How to Solve It," Brandeis dwelled extensively on the theme of America as a nation composed of different nationalities. The free and creative development of these nationalities would spiritually enrich the United States and would make it a democracy *par excellence*, he claimed. This address of Brandeis became a hallmark of mainstream American Zionism, secular and religious alike.[7]

Another feature of Brandeis's Zionism, expressing his genuine American path to Jewish nationalism, was his conceiving of Zionism as a means for attaining higher goals. His short speech accepting the chairmanship of the Provisional Executive Committee for General Zionist Affairs (August 30, 1914) classically reflected this mission orientation.

> Experiences, public and professional, have taught me this: I find Jews possessed of those very qualities which we of the twentieth century seek to develop in our struggle for justice and democracy; a deep moral feeling which makes them capable of noble acts; a deep sense of the brotherhood of man; and a high intelligence, the fruit of three thousand years of civilization. These experiences have made me feel that the Jewish people have something which should be saved for the world; that the Jewish people should be preserved; and that this is our duty to pursue that method of saving which most promises success.[8]

The mission-orientation of Brandeis's Zionism did not single him out from other Americanized Zionists. Actually, a thread of a mission rationale ran through American Zionism since its foundation. The first president of the Federation of American Zionists, Richard Gottheil (1898-1904), expounded the idea; and subsequent Zionist leaders, secular and religious alike, similarly expressed a mission rationale for their Zionism. Zionist personalities of different backgrounds, such as Henry P. Mendes, Judah Magnes, Horace Kallen, and Henrietta Szold, largely rationalized Zionism by the potential contribution to mankind of the movement and the future state. Indeed, suggesting the creation of a new state against many heavy odds required, in the American context, a justification meaningful also for society at large. It was the mission rationale that fulfilled this requirement.[9]

The mission-orientation of Brandeis's Zionism was, however, especially pronounced. Both the American and the Progressive in him did not let him adopt Zionism without a conspicuous general rationale. A third factor that worked to intensify his mission-orientation was his Puritan urge. This Puritan element previously referred to was a main characteristic of Brandeis's Zionism during the phase discussed in this chapter. His Zionist addresses during this phase were bound to Puritan ideals and were immersed in Puritan images. He often spoke in those years, for example, about "our Pilgrim ancestors" when pointing to the first pioneers who had come to Palestine. It was the bold spirit of the early Puritans that he found among the Jewish settlers, and it was the formers' success that he time and again brought as a promise. Moreover, the Puritan bent and the mission-orientation of Brandeis were interwoven in the vein of the Puritan tradition to establish a model society, "a City upon a Hill." In his bitter conflict with the European Zionists (in the early twenties) about the way to build Palestine, Brandeis said: "Our aim is the Kingdom of Heaven, paraphrasing Cromwell. We take Palestine by the way. But we must take it with clean hands; we must take it in a way as to ennoble the Jewish people. Otherwise, it will not be worth having."[10]

A good part of Brandeis's attitudes in that historic conflict should be traced to the Puritan-like source of his Zionism. His zealous passion for self-reliance of the Yishuv, his detestation for and fear of any resemblance to the *Chalukkah* system were Puritan in nature. In the same pattern were also his obsession for very high standards of work ethic, strict accountability, and rigorous scrupulousness in general. In sum, Brandeis of the twenties expected the Yishuv to develop much along the lines of the cherished Puritan saga.[11]

European Zionism was a movement for an all-embracing—culture, language, historical traditions—nationalist renaissance. Brandeis's brand, however, focused, in keeping with his own ethnic development, on the building up of Palestine along certain social-ethical values. Immigration to Palestine was suitable for the unfortunate European brethren and for the few American pioneers; and cultural renewal, again, was limited (from the nationalist point of view) in Brandeis's version of Zionism to upholding sublime values. In this kind of Palestinian endeavor, Brandeis believed, sympathetic non-Zionists and Zionists could most closely cooperate. He thus suggested that an organization, about equally shared by interested non-Zionists and Zionists, would lead the building of Palestine. This concept, alongside his Puritan vision, was a major cause for his bitter conflict with the European Zionists, headed by Chaim Weizmann, in the years 1919-29.[12]

Great Britain controlled Palestine from the end of 1917 (to the establishment of Israel), and Zionists of all countries had, of course, to take a stand in the face of this reality. Actually, the attitude toward the British Mandate (1920-48) became a touchstone for the various Zionist ideologies.

Brandeis's attitude toward Britain during that period derived largely from his Puritan element. He admired Britain as the great bearer of the Anglo-Saxon ethic; that country embodied for him the values he most cherished, such as economic creativity, democracy, and education. He loved London and wrote amiably about the English people. When it came to virtues of character, thought Brandeis, both "America and Great Britain excel"; and he admired "their superiority in moral, mental, and physical cleanliness." "Cleanliness" meant for him exactitude, industry, high regard for science, as well as purity and fairness.[13]

As the Mandatory power of Palestine, Britain was committed by its own declaration and by international law to establish a Jewish national home in Palestine. Brandeis was predisposed to trust British policies. Moreover, of Puritan mentality, he highly regarded promises especially when legalized. Brandeis adhered to this attitude throughout his first Zionist phase, roughly the years 1914-29.

Brandeis's attitude becomes clearer when compared with that of Vladimir Ze'ev Jabotinsky, the European Zionist thinker and future leader of the nationalistic Revisionist movement. (The Revionist party was founded in 1925 and demanded that the entire mandated territory of Palestine on both sides of the Jordan River be turned into a Jewish state. Hostile to progressive and labor Zionism, in 1935 the Revisionists seceded from the World Zionist Organization and established the New Zionist Organization.) The two personalities met for the first time in Palestine in 1919. This was, however, also their last meeting as it opened a rift that kept them apart until the end of their lives. The historic encounter is related by Jabotinsky's biographer.

> When Jabotinsky met Justice Brandeis, he told him plainly that the [British] administration's policy was bound to result in anti-Jewish outbreaks and did not shrink from using the word "pogrom." . . . When Jabotinsky told him: "We of Russian origin are like hunting dogs who can smell blood from afar," Brandeis answered: "Why do you quote examples from Russia? This is not Tsarist Russia. This is a territory occupied by an Anglo-Saxon Power. It belongs to a completely different world. I do believe in British justice." When Jabotinksy continued . . . Brandeis replied coldly: "Sir, I can only see that we do not speak a common language."[14]

The early and decisive breach between Brandeis and Jabotinsky clearly reflected the American peculiarities of the former's Zionism. The American Zionist leader trusted the Anglo-Saxon power as he considered it playing according to a special set of rules; this "completely different world," Brandeis believed, would enable some sort of a clean way to fulfill the dream. He judged Zionist policies not as a mundane effort amid power-hungry countries but rather as a means to cleanly pursue lofty goals. Thus, he felt threatened by Jabotinsky's course that might profane his "Kingdom of Heaven" vision and the ennobling way toward it—hence the zealousness for his own attitude and the early and total rejection of Jabotinsky's.

Neither the decisive breach with Jabotinsky nor the conflict with Weizmann meant that Brandeis was closed to the influence of other Zionist thinkers. He integrated other influences, however, into his own mind-set. There was a relationship between the two major Zionist schools at the time—political Zionism and cultural Zionism—and the Zionist thought of Brandeis.

Through his early loyal assistant in Zionist affairs, Jacob de Haas, Brandeis came to know the work of the founder of political Zionism, Theodor Herzl. Brandeis tended to accept the Herzlian line of relying on international legal arrangements to assure the development of Jewish Palestine; this line was in harmony with his own attitude that inclined to emphasize the significance of international legal commitments. However, Brandeis totally disregarded other aspects of Herzlian Zionism, for example, Herzl's vision of ingathering all the exiles in Palestine as the ultimate goal of the movement.[15]

Similarly, Brandeis was attracted to Ahad Ha'am, prime expounder of cultural Zionism, according to which the development of Jewish culture and spiritual values should be at the core of Jewish nationalism. He did not share, though, the European Zionist's passion for cultural self-realization nor his love for nationalist historical traditions. What Brandeis did appreciate in Ahad Ha'amism became clear in his letter to the Zionist philosopher in September 1917 (with the approaching of the Balfour Declaration). "I . . . acknowledge my great indebtedness [to you]. Unfortunately I cannot read your writings in the original. Of the history and other things Jewish I was almost as ignorant as of this language. Your essays gave me some understanding and revealed to me that much which I ignorantly worshiped was my own." Obviously, the reference was to social justice that Ahad Ha'am considered as central to the Jewish ethos.[16]

About a year later Brandeis wrote to Ahad Ha'am, "With the approaching realization of our dreams, I am prompted to thank again our great teachers, to whom I owe so much." He continued to praise Ahad Ha'am's legacy, implying that its essence was commitment to democracy and justice. The European Zionist philosopher, on the other hand, emphasized justice as an organic part of a Hebrew-speaking Jewish society well versed in the prophetic tradition.[17]

Brandeis's interest in Judaism was indeed confined by his conspicuously American kind of Zionism. First, his attention focused on social-ethical values he considered applicable to the modern world. Second, he tended to concentrate on tenets and accomplishments of diaspora Jewish history. From time to time, he added to the list of qualities to adopt in his above-quoted August 1914 speech. In his "Duty of Educated Jews" (November 1914, Intercollegiate Menorah Association, Columbia University), he listed the following: intellectual capacity; an appreciation of the value of education; indomitable will; capacity for hard work; and again, above all, the quest for democracy and justice. As to the practice of democracy among Jews, he stressed "an all pervading sense of duty in the citizen"; "submission to leadership as distinguished from authority"; and "a developed community sense."[18]

Recalling Brandeis's path to Judaism and Zionism, it's not surprising that he always found deep kinship, even identity, between American and Jewish ideals. In the above-mentioned Menorah address, for example, he claimed "that the twentieth century ideals of America have been the ideals of the Jew for more than twenty centuries." He succinctly summarized his concept in "The Rebirth of the Jewish Nation" speech of September 1914. "Jews were by reason of their traditions and their character peculiarly fitted in the attainment of American ideals. . . . to be good Americans, we must be better Jews, and to be better Jews, we must become Zionists."[19]

America in the twenties and traumatic events beyond its borders in 1929-30 and in subsequent years reshaped Brandeis's

Zionist ideology. Classic Brandeisian Zionism, a distinctive result of the American circumstances in the Progressive era, was confronted by new phenomena and was tested by world processes, some of which touched the American shores as well. Brandeis, ever too realistic and too humanistic to be dogmatic, responded creatively to the new realities.

Post–World War I America was pervaded by chauvinsim and intolerance. Calvin Coolidge's dictum—"America must be kept American"—set the tone of the decade and beyond. The United States was inhospitable then to even the vaguest version of cultural pluralism. These circumstances caused Brandeis's Zionism to be almost exclusively concentrated on Palestine. Inherent tendencies in his own original Zionist posture also worked to this effect; the reduction of Judaism and Zionism to values shared with American democracy did not leave much room for a distinctive Jewish life in the diaspora. The noble Jewish ideals, virtually identified in his eyes with the ideals of American Progressives, could be a part of a special Jewish civilization chiefly beyond the diaspora. These built-in ideological tendencies of Brandeis's Zionism were now strengthened by the rejectionist factors of America in the twenties. The result was that the Jewish endeavor in Palestine, the building up there of a model society, clearly came to be the dominant characteristics of Brandeisian American Zionism.[20]

During the twenties nativism in this country ran high; one of its expressions was the Sacco and Vanzetti affair in which the Brandeis family was closely involved. The United States drastically changed its immigration laws, obviously discriminating against Catholics and Jews. Anti-Semitism became a persistent and a considerable force in the United States (until the end of World War II).

Post–World War I Europe became less hospitable than ever for Jews; and in different types of countries, ranging from agrarian Poland to industrialized and "highly cultured" Germany, the danger of a most brutal anti-Semitism became imminent. Brandeis was highly sensitive regarding developments in Germany. He bitingly condemned the evasive attitudes of assimilated German Jews (in Germany as well as in the United States). And during the first week of Hitler's regime, he stated: "They [Germany's Jews] must all leave. All of them. There is no other way." When Rabbi Stephen Wise asked him how 600,000 people could be taken out of Germany, Brandeis repeated: "They must all leave. I would have the Jews out of Germany. They have been treated with the deepest disrespect. I urge that Germany shall be free of Jews. Let Germany share the fate of Spain [from which all Jews had been expelled in 1492]. No Jew must live in Germany."[21]

Brandeis supported many of the activities of Stephen Wise who had early faced the peril of growing Nazism and who courageously worked to mobilize American public opinion, Jewish and non-Jewish, to thwart the danger.[22]

Though Brandeis had made a few comments on anti-Semitism during the twenties, it was in 1930 that he summed up the menacing processes in a clear-cut, conclusive way. In a programmatic letter to Robert Szold, his loyal assistant in Zionist matters, he then incisively concluded:

> The condition of the Jews in the Diaspora in 1930—as compared with 1920 and 1914—has worsened to such a degree, that the belief of thinking Jews that the Jewish problem would be solved by growing enlightenment in the Diaspora must have been seriously shaken—if not shattered. . . .
>
> The anti-Semitic outbreaks in Europe, the closing of the doors to immigrants by practically all the new countries, the rise of anti-Semitism even in the new countries remove the old alternatives from consideration. The question now presented largely is Palestine—or Despair?[23]

In Brandeis's eyes Palestine now stood first of all as a haven for the despaired; this role gradually came to overshadow the old one assigned by him to Palestine—that of being a social laboratory in the service of democracy and progressivism. In 1930 the very fact that the gates of Palestine were open for the Jews gave that country the crucially needed humanistic function. In an alienated and cruel world, only the Jewish homeland presented itself as a refuge for the persecuted people.

The situation of the Yishuv itself also worked to reshape Brandeis's classic Zionist concept. Arab leadership from the twenties on resorted to terrorist tactics in its attempts to hamper Zionist activity in Palestine. Hajj Amin al-Husayni, mufti of Jerusalem, instigated Muslim fanaticism and Arab-Palestinian brutal chauvinism aimed against the whole Jewish population in Palestine. A future collaborator of Hitler, al-Husayni directed in the summer of 1929 a murderous attack aimed to terrorize the whole Yishuv (over one hundred Jews were killed and four hundred were injured). This attack brought from Brandeis a new kind of reaction (compared, for example, with his careful criticism of Arab violence in 1921). He detested and was deeply alarmed by the chauvinist-terrorist attack. Concerned for Jewish Palestine's security, he determined to listen most attentively to the leaders of the Yishuv's defense reports, to respect their judgments, and to lavishly furnish assistance for security purposes.[24]

Palestine as a refuge for Jews from persecuting countries was always an element in Brandeis's Zionism, but now the perspective was different. The danger for European Jewry was imminent; and the "place of refuge" itself, Jewish Palestine, was savagely threatened. Brandeis now felt a new kind of responsibility, grave and clearly nationalist, of safeguarding the physical survival of his people. The mission rationale of his Zionism now retreated, and a survivalist motif came to the fore.

A new image of the Yishuv now began to force itself upon his mind. A courageous, self-defending settlement strategically located on the top of the hill gradually replaced the previous vision of a model city of justice upon a hill. His fighting-back brethren in Palestine instilled in him a mix of new pride and concern. In a letter (September 1929) to Felix Frankfurter, Brandeis emphasized the need to enable the Yishuv to defend itself. "As against the Bedouins, our pioneers are in a position not unlike the American settlers against the Indians. I saw myself the need of their self-defense in 1919 in Poreah, with our Shomer [watchman], on guard mounted on the hill top, and the blacktented Bedouins below who had peaceably but with ever robber purpose, crossed the Jordan." And to this he immediately added, "As to other Arabs, the position is not different in essence, of course."[25]

Brandeis of the thirties was thrilled when he learned that Palestinian Jews were "good fighters," and he loved retelling stories about settlers who managed to defend their villages heroically against Arab attackers. Again, survivalism, though still somewhat tinted with the old Puritan colors, became a major theme.[26]

British policies in Palestine also worked to realign Brandeis's original Zionist ideas. In March 1930 the Report of the Commission on the Palestine Disturbances of August 1929 was published, ushering in a new era in relations between the Zionist movement and the Mandate government. The report cast doubt on the ability of the Zionist movement to settle more Jews in Palestine without dispossessing Arabs. Whereas direct blame for the riots was attributed to the Arabs, the committee found "mitigating circumstances" in the conduct of the Jews. In the months after the publication of the report, the British government policy became increasingly hostile toward the emergent National Home, and immigration quotas were curtailed to the point of actual suspension. In October 1930 the Passfield White Paper was published, sanctioning anti-Zionist policies. Brandeis was very active in the partly successful effort to repeal this policy. The whole experience, however, was somewhat traumatic for him. The British could no longer be counted on as the bearers of the Anglo-Saxon ethos. For him this was not merely a case of a change of policies but "a betrayal"; England ignored both legal commitments and the rules of fair play. The civilized Anglo-Saxon country demolished rules of the game he had sacredly believed in. Consequently, he turned "inward," to an appreciation of Jewish political self-reliance and activism.[27]

It was in this vein of Brandeis's growing Zionist militancy that "his people" contributed to the revolt that deposed philo-British Chaim Weizmann from the presidency of the World Zionist Organization at the 1931 Zionist Congress. Maybe this was in part a personal vendetta (in retaliation for the deposition of the Brandeisian leadership of the ZOA [Zionist Organization of America] by the pro-Weizmannites in the Cleveland convention of 1921); but mainly it was a demonstration of a new line, of an evolution of Brandeis's original Zionism. He now painfully learned that self-interest was a basic rule of "the game of nations," England included. His Zionism, in response, became both more worldly and more militant.[28]

In conclusion, several factors worked to revise Brandeis's mission-oriented Zionism: nativism and anti-Semitism in the United States; chauvinism, Nazism, and brutal anti-Semitism in Europe; Arab Palestinian terrorism; the beginning of Britain's retreat from the Mandate. All these factors combined to dilute the mission rationale of Brandeis's Zionism. His Zionism was now seriously attuned to assuring the very existence of the Jewish people. With the attenuation of the mission justification, Brandeis's Zionism became somewhat somber and more nationalistic.

Brandeis's new Zionist approach was also expressed in a change in his policy of giving. Actually, his financial contributions always reflected, and often very accurately so, the significance he attributed to certain causes. As has been noted elsewhere, his contributions to the Boston Jewish philanthropic organizations sensitively registered his growing interest in Judaism and Zionism. During the twenties (when the conflict with the Weizmannites on the method of building Palestine was at its height), Brandeis's contributions to Palestine were carefully selective and relatively modest. During the period 1925-29, his contributions to the Zionist movement totaled about $30,000. In a dramatic increase, he gave in 1930 alone almost $40,000. During the ensuing years, he maintained this extremely high level of assistance.[29] Brandeis himself rationalized his new approach by claiming (in the summer of 1930) that during the last decade the Yishuv had overcome the economic blurs of the past; he claimed that the Yishuv was now bound toward self-reliance and was appealing to productive people from abroad to join.[30]

In other words, Brandeis rationalized that the Yishuv passed the high Puritan test and that it therefore deserved lavish economic support. More than an assumed change in the economic ways of the Yishuv, I would suggest it was the aforementioned events and processes and the change of Brandeis's own attitude that brought about his dramatically greater help. Together with his huge contributions, Brandeis very much intensified his interest in the details of Palestine's development. His in-depth knowledge regarding Palestine became legendary and amazed even the most "inside" Palestinian Jews. Revealingly, he then began to talk about the "happiness" of the Zionists working in Palestine, and he found them "achieving a degree of happiness not experienced elsewhere." Undoubtedly, the psychological term employed and the affirmative conclusions reflected Brandeis's own eagerness and clear inclination to uninhibitedly identify with the enterprise in the Jewish homeland.[31]

Along with the new nationalist disposition, there naturally developed a discernment and an appreciation of the dynamic forces in the Yishuv. And the leading element, throughout the twenties (and virtually until the establishment of Israel), proved to be the labor movement with its accomplishments in the economy, settlement, and self-defense (Hagannah, the precursor of the Israel Defense Forces, was founded and led by the Labor movement). Already in the late twenties, Brandeis began to support the Histadruth, the General Federation of Hebrew Workers in Palestine; but this was then sporadic and largely philanthropic support. Conspicuous expressions of Brandeis's new course came during 1930 when he entrusted the Palestine Economic Council and the Palestine Economic Corporation with extremely large building projects and others connected with the cooperative movement in Palestine. He then made arrangements to be directly and systematically updated. In the summer of that year, Brandeis began to cultivate a network of people who would be experts on the labor economy in Palestine and who would professionally help the advancement of the cooperative movement. He considered the success of the Histadruth sector—in his eyes, the backbone of striving Jewish Palestine—crucial for the whole Zionist endeavor.[32]

Beginning in the mid-thirties, a political alliance emerged

between Brandeis and the leadership of the Labor camp in Palestine, especially David Ben-Gurion, the previously militant Histadruth leader. In a comprehensive letter (January 1934), Ben-Gurion reported to Brandeis on his recent visit to London and his analysis of the world scene. He predicted that both Germany and Japan were preparing for a world war. The only feasible solution for the Jews, he wrote, was Palestine; and the experience of fifty years of agricultural pioneering proved that the land could absorb tremendously more Jews than the British were willing to admit. The only plan open to the Zionists, he concluded, was to continue their work in Palestine, creating a national home designed to absorb masses of Jews. Brandeis responded to this document in a decisively positive manner. "I agree entirely with the opinion which you express, with the reasons therefor, and that we should strive unceasingly to obtain the objective stated. I believe this is possible. So far as may be possible, I shall lend aid." In a letter (June 1936), aimed against the anti–Ben-Gurion criticism of some "dovish" circles, Brandeis made his opinion known. "We have in Ben-Gurion and [Moshe] Shertock [Sharett, head of the political department of the Jewish Agency] practical leaders of great ability, men of understanding, vision and wisdom rare in government. We should give them unqualified, ardent support."[33]

A member of the Jewish Agency for Palestine's Executive since 1933 and its chairman since 1935, Ben-Gurion increasingly questioned Weizmann's traditional philo-British line. From 1938 he came to cultivate an Anglo-American orientation instead, relying heavily on arousing American public opinion. Gradually, Ben-Gurion came to be Brandeis's political ally in a Zionist alignment, loose though it was, often arrayed against Weizmann and his followers. High points of the Brandeis–Ben-Gurion relation came when the latter assured, in May–June 1935, massive support of Brandeis for the development of the strategic port of Akaba (now Elath, on the northeastern arm of the Red Sea, at the southern end of the Negev) and when Brandeis firmly backed Ben-Gurion's militant policy against the forthcoming anti-Zionist British White Paper policy in January 1939. Though during 1940-41 Brandeis did not always adhere to Ben-Gurion's militant course, he did pursue a line that was much akin to that of the dynamic Palestinian leader.[34]

To reiterate, Brandeis's Zionist ideology of the years 1914-29 was mission oriented, advocated cultural pluralism, and was immersed in Puritanic ideals and images. But from about 1930, his nationalist outlook became primarily survivalist oriented; it focused almost exclusively on the Palestinian scene, and it emerged from its Puritanic vicarious nature. Symbolically, beginning in the early thirties, Brandeis began for the first time to use the Hebrew word *halutz* (pioneer; plural—*halutzim*). This terminology, along with his avoidance of the old philo-Yankee phraseology, reflected Brandeis's new Zionist affirmation. He now wholeheartedly identified with the embattled pilgrims of his own people.

Who were those *halutzim* with whom Brandeis now fully identified? They were *not* chiefly good fighters. Actually, most of them saw the war in general as a terrible evil and their embattled situation in Palestine as tragic and imposed upon them by external circumstances. They took pride not in military feats, necessary as they were for their self-defense, but rather in building. And they worked not merely to build up a modern national economy in a desolated country but also to create at the same time a new society.[35] Indeed, it is, therefore, imperative to examine Brandeis's new Zionist version in the context of social Palestine. But before doing this, we should return for a moment to Brandeis the Progressive. And we should emphasize that he firmly retained his social-ethical beliefs and idealism to the end of his life.

Brandeis was disgusted by the developments in American society and its economy during the twenties. A central figure in this development was the true New Englander Calvin Coolidge, vice-president from 1921 to 1923 and president from 1923 to 1929. In a candid letter to Frankfurter, Brandeis revealed how "painful, distressful and depressing" it was for him to listen to Coolidge and that he regarded this thoroughly business-oriented president as systematically working to deprive America of all its idealism. When he tried to recall the next

most depressing and distressful experience of his lifetime,
wrote Brandeis, he had to go back over thirty years, when in
preparing for the Public Institutions Hearings, he had gone
to a Boston's Poor-House hospital and had passed through
the syphilitic ward. "I had a like sense of uncleanness," he
gloomily wrote to his friend.[36]

With these deep feelings of aversion, it was not surprising
Brandeis looked abroad for new horizons and cleaner air. During the earlier period of his disenchantment with the Yankees,
he had begun a serious acquaintance with British Labor. This
time, as a result of the materialistic twenties and the depression of 1929-33, he began to be intensely interested in Denmark's democratic socialism. Since the early thirties, he was
eagerly learning about the Danish cooperative system and
energetically publicizing it.[37]

In Brandeis's mind Palestine also held great social promise
similar to that of Denmark. Already in the Zionist Organization of America's Pittsburgh Program of 1918, of which he
was a mentor, there was a call to apply the cooperative principle "so far as feasible in the organization of agricultural,
industrial, commercial, and financial undertakings." Actually, Jewish Palestine advanced along lines similar to the
progressive course recommended by the Pittsburgh Program;
and it developed a dynamic and socially most interesting and
diverse cooperative sector. Already in 1923 the Histadruth set
up the Cooperative Society (Hevrat Ha-Ovdim), which embraced all the cooperative enterprises in Palestine with the
purpose of shaping the Jewish homeland as a democratic-
cooperative society.[38] It was, however, only at the end of the
twenties that this unique social endeavor was definitely appreciated by Brandeis. In his aforementioned pro-Histadruth
letter of the summer of 1930 to Robert Szold, he wrote: "The
social life and strivings of the [Palestinian] Jews . . . affords
abundant material for appeal to Jewish liberals—with or
without religious faith and to idealists of any race or
creed. . . . The aspirations and striving of the Jewish Labor
Organization, [i.e., the Histadruth] and the achievements
should appeal mightily to our progressives." Brandeis came
to support financially some cooperative enterprises. Politically

more significant was the fact that he sustained dailies and periodicals of mainstream labor Zionism in Hebrew, English, and Arabic.[39]

The previous section showed that Brandeis's orientation toward the Histadruth derived in large measure from his understanding that this was the national pioneering and most reliable camp. To this must now be added that his interest in the labor sector in Palestine should be interpreted in the light of his progressivism as well.

Within labor Palestine, the kibbutz federation Ha-Shomer Ha-Tzair pointedly enchanted Louis Brandeis. The social and the national ideology of this youth movement was marked by radicalism: negation of the diaspora, rejection of the established social order, and formation of a kibbutz network in Palestine. Alongside deep dedication to the Hebrew culture, efforts were made to synthesize Zionism and revolutionary socialism. The radicalism of Ha-Shomer Ha-Tzair had additional distinctive features relevant to this discussion: The movement fostered among its adherents a search for the root of things and a demand for consistency of thought, analysis, and action; this led to the principal obligation of the individual—that of personal fulfillment of ideals and conclusions. A sophisticated educational system created a pioneering atmosphere in Ha-Shomer Ha-Tzair groups, and pedagogic measures culminated in the obligation to make *aliyah* (immigration to Palestine) and to live in a kibbutz. The movement was detached from the traditions of the European *shtetl* (small town) perhaps more than the other kibbutz trends, emphasized efficiency, and was noted for its "delivering-the-goods" frame of mind. Finally, paramount emphasis was placed in Ha-Shomer Ha-Tzair upon educating the whole person—moral development, building capacity for collective action, strengthening of character, work ethic, resourcefulness, self-discipline, and austerity.[40]

The historic figure in the Brandeis–Ha-Shomer Ha-Tzair connection was Irma Lindheim, president of Hadassah from 1926 to 1928, an intimate ally of Brandeis in the American Zionist battles, and an admirer of the radical Zionist movement. In her autobiography she relates the beginning of the

Brandeis–Ha-Shomer Ha-Tzair relationship. It was about 1930
when she was in Detroit and first met a Ha-Shomer Ha-Tzair
youth group. The Hadassah leader "was struck by the extraordinary level of their intellect, culture and purposefulness."
And she was even more deeply impressed by their being an
antidote to the corrupted twenties and by their Puritan-like,
yet modern, qualities. "Here were young people, virile, modern, spirited, utterly immune to the allure of law-breaking
which seemed in the very air of the times, adhering with utter
naturalness to abstinence from liquor, and even from smok-
ing, which was also against their code."

> It was after this visit, and similar experiences in Boston,
> Montreal, and elsewhere [relates Irma Lindheim], that
> I took occasion to visit Mr. Brandeis in Washington. I
> wanted to discuss with him my discovery of this group
> of young people who were fitting themselves for lives
> according to principles which were his own.
>   Ever a man who admired people who lived by their
> beliefs, he listened closely, a brooding yet gratified
> expression in his eyes, to what I had to tell him of the
> youth movement. He put searching questions. . . .
> Judge Brandeis asked if I thought it would be possible
> for him to meet some of the young people themselves,
> to hear from their own lips of their dreams, hopes, plans.
> It struck me that he was reaching out to live vicariously
> what might, had the opportunity come earlier in his life,
> have become a fulfillment he could have wished for him-
> self.[41]

Lindheim then introduced Mordecai Bentov to Brandeis.
A member of kibbutz Mishmar Ha-Emek, a thinker and a
leader of the movement, Bentov was a Ha-Shomer Ha-Tzair
delegate to the United States between 1931 and 1933. (Upon
the establishment of the State of Israel, he became its minister
of labor and reconstruction.) A spiritual rapport and warm
personal relations developed between the young, intellectual
kibbutz member and Justice Brandeis.[42]
    On the verge of his departure to Palestine, Mordecai Bentov

wrote a thoughtful letter to Brandeis, summarizing their interaction. In an idealistic vein, he dwelled on the values of
hard work and self-reliance that were central to the movement
he represented. This movement, he also stressed, was a ful-
filling one—ideals and professed values had to be realized
either through personal behavior or through communal effort.
Bentov's letter vividly depicted a movement that was devoted
to physical work but also pursued education and cultural life.
Finally, in a simple and dignified way, the writer expressed
his high regard for Brandeis—as a Progressive, a Zionist, and
an inspiring idealist.[43]

Upon returning to his kibbutz, Bentov wrote a six-page
ideological letter to Brandeis that demonstrated again the kinship that had developed between the two men. Individualism,
reflected the kibbutz theoretician, was a most cherished value
in his movement; the cooperative system, he suggested, was
both the best basis for pursuing individualism as well as the
guarantee for the development of a refined personal character.
He wrote explicitly about the "pioneer ideals and puritan morals of the New Palestine," and described how the humanistic
nature of the kibbutz society enabled it to overcome the natural hardships that surrounded it.[44]

There was also an interesting political-economic facet to
this letter of the Ha-Shomer Ha-Tzair ideologue. While his
kibbutz movement was committed to a high work ethic and
to the principles of efficiency, the movement's development
was hampered by high interest on loans. The banks, wrote
Bentov to the author of *Other People's Money*, should be tamed
to serve the productive, hardworking elements of society.[45]

There was not much concrete political content in Bentov's
letters to Brandeis. The subject that did emerge clearly—and
undoubtedly was shared by both of them—was a firm opposition to fascism abroad and to Revisionism at home.[46]

The letter ended with a detailed account of the first American group that was then in Palestine preparing itself to establish a kibbutz. Bentov mentioned his "old idea of having
them [the American *halutzim*] settled on land adjoining Mishmar Ha-Emek."[47] As will be shown, that idea did materialize,
and an "American" Ha-Shomer Ha-Tzair kibbutz was estab-

lished not far from Bentov's and was named after Justice Louis D. Brandeis.

The emissary of Ha-Shomer Ha-Tzair in the United States in the late thirties was Joshua Leibner. He carried on Bentov's educational endeavor and was, thanks to his *halutzic* and puristic character, very warmly appreciated by Brandeis. It is instructive to note that it was during the time of Leibner, who was an educational (rather than a political) personality, that the connection between Ha-Shomer Ha-Tzair and Brandeis was conclusively cemented.[48]

Joshua Leibner was one of the founders of the "American" kibbutz named after Brandeis. Established in 1937 on the Menasheh Hills, it was called Ein Ha-Shofet (in Hebrew, The Spring of the Judge). Shmuel Ben-Zvi, another founder of the new kibbutz, served as a representative of Ha-Shomer Ha-Tzair in America from 1940 to 1946. He met Brandeis both in Washington and in his Chatham summer house and kept alive Brandeis's connection with Ein Ha-Shofet and Ha-Shomer Ha-Tzair. Brandeis himself—with love, concern, and admiration—followed up and supported the development of the pioneering communal settlement.[49]

When Britain published the anti-Zionist White Paper of May 1939, Brandeis swiftly responded. He volunteered to support the founding of another Ha-Shomer Ha-Tzair kibbutz (near Ein Ha-Shofet). "Such action might help to make them understand where our faith lies," he wrote. Eventually, the other kibbutz was established in 1941 and was named Ramat Ha-Shofet (The Height of the Judge) in honor of Julian W. Mack (earlier Brandeis's closest ally in Zionist matters).[50]

Significantly, Brandeis supported not just "his" kibbutz but all the activity of the Ha-Shomer Ha-Tzair movement in the United States.[51] This and his initiative to establish another Ha-Shomer Ha-Tzair kibbutz testify to the depth and the constancy of his attraction to Ha-Shomer Ha-Tzair.

What qualities of Ha-Shomer Ha-Tzair appealed to Brandeis? How far did ideology and politics play a role in this connection?

It is not in the strictly political dimension that one should look for an explanation of the connection between Brandeis

and the radical kibbutz movement. The Marxist-socialist leanings of Ha-Shomer Ha-Tzair and the growing sympathy for
Soviet Russia and—in regard to Zionist policies—the inclination to a binational solution of the Arab-Jewish conflict all
certainly ran against Brandeis's beliefs.

That world of differences, however, should not obscure
the significance of the Brandeis–Ha-Shomer Ha-Tzair connection. Even in the political sphere, it seems that there was
a formidable link between the Progressive-American and the
Socialist-Zionist movement, namely, a detestation for and
firm stand against Revisionism.[52] But, again, the kernel of the
connection lay beyond politics.

Irma Lindheim, who eventually joined kibbutz Mishmar
Ha-Emek, sensed that the Ha-Shomer Ha-Tzair kind of pioneer life such as that of Joshua Leibner was for Brandeis the
ultimate realization of his ideals. Philip S. Bernstein, the noted
social-minded religious leader who was the Brandeises' neigh-
bor and frequent visitor in Cape Cod, corroborates Lindheim's
firsthand impressions. In his memoirs on Louis Brandeis, he
states, "I try to recall the individuals of whom he [Brandeis]
spoke highly"; and here he lists a few leaders in American
Jewish life and Zionism and concludes, "However, his greatest enthusiasm was reserved for unknown young men, like
Joshua Leibner of Ha-Shomer Ha-Tzair, in whom he found
the healthiest combination of American pioneer spirit, Jewish
idealism, and social vision."[53] The firsthand impressions and
direct observations of Lindheim and Bernstein seem to have
much validity.

Indeed, it was the educational-ideological traits of Ha-
Shomer Ha-Tzair that attracted Brandeis. It has been shown
that in the process of the intensification of his Zionism the
mission rationale attenuated significantly and that he gradually ceased to identify with the Pilgrims as his revered ancestors. He now needed a new group with which to identify.
This group had to be socially compassionate; had to integrate
boldly the nationalist drive into a broader social-ethical endeavor; had to be conspicuously idealistic, pioneering, and
of Puritan qualities; had to be far enough from the shtetl's
slovenly style to represent modernity and efficiency; and had

to emphasize Jewish values rather than tradition. The Ha-Shomer Ha-Tzair movement—which in great measure exemplified these traits—came to serve as the object of Brandeis's search for identity. It was the *halutzim* of kibbutzim such as Mishmar Ha-Emek, Ein Ha-Shofet, and Ramat Ha-Shofet that obviously appealed to his social-ethical and idealistic impulses and to his search for a meaningful Jewish identity.

An interesting expression of Brandeis's progressive-Zionism and his attraction to the Ha-Shomer Ha-Tzair type of people was his support of the American Zionist students' organization, Avukah (Torch). Officially affiliated with the Zionist Organization of America (ZOA), which subsidized its activities, Avukah retained from its inception an ideological orientation of labor Zionism. During the thirties, under the leadership of people such as Zellig Harris (of the University of Pennsylvania, president of Avukah from 1934 to the end of the thirties) and the younger Seymour Melman (of the City College of New York and Columbia University), the organization became increasingly radical. Accusations were made that the movement was preoccupied with general American issues rather than with Jewish ones; that it concentrated on the American scene instead of on Palestine; and that it adhered to Marxist philosophy and had procommunist leanings. Beginning in the late thirties, the relationship between Avukah and the ZOA was extremely strained. (As a result of this conflict and America's participation in World War II—army service claimed more and more of the Avukah membership— Avukah's New York headquarters was permanently closed in 1943.)[54]

At its 1938 convention, Avukah adopted a "three-fronts" program to which it adhered during the subsequent years. According to Avukah's analysis, American Jewry suffered chronically from a minority situation, was ever threatened by fascism and anti-Semitism, and in any case did not have much to offer to its enlightened youth. Avukah's solution was twofold: outward—a bold struggle for civil liberties conducted together with antifascist and progressive forces; and inward— a radical democratization of American Jewry's communal structure. On the "third front"—Palestine—Avukah's *Program for American Jews* hailed the Yishuv as "a progressive society, free . . . from some of the general social ills that beset the western world." Avukah explicitly called for the Labor Zionists to retain their leadership in the building up of Palestine. Moreover, the student organization clearly implied in its program that it was the Ha-Shomer Ha-Tzair movement that was best qualified to fulfill the vision of a new society in the Jewish homeland.[55]

Indeed, the students' organization, under Harris's leadership, adopted all the major political tenets of Ha-Shomer Ha-Tzair. Also, Avukah of the late thirties and early forties cultivated very close practical connections as well as fast personal relations with the radical kibbutz movement. The close relations of Avukah with Ha-Shomer Ha-Tzair expanded in both the United States and in Palestine. Kibbutz Ein Ha-Shofet (the one named after Brandeis) served Avukah as a base for the organization's Palestinian programs.[56]

Brandeis was consistently interested in the work of Avukah, supported it financially, and met regularly with the organization's leaders and activists. Zellig Harris, a compassionate Progressive-Zionist whom the justice very much appreciated, visited Brandeis quite often. When Harris quit his official positions in Avukah in 1939-40, Brandeis asked him to be informally involved in the organization's affairs. Harris responded affirmatively and retained his influence. Despite repeated accusations of Avukah's ultraleftist leanings, Brandeis maintained his support of the organization to his last days.[57]

What attracted Brandeis to the radical students' organization and made him its constant supporter? The answer may, to an important degree, lie in the political arena. While Ha-Shomer Ha-Tzair was chiefly a pioneering and educational movement, Avukah was mainly a political-ideological organization. A major feature that distinguished Avukah under Zellig Harris's leadership was its militant anti-Revisionist stance. Actually, the very emergence of Harris to leadership and his whole Avukah career were characterized by his firm attitude against Revisionism. In the summer of 1934, he devoted himself to holding off the Revisionists' attempt to get control, in ways he considered nondemocratic, of the American Zionist student organization. He then began systematically to learn about fascism in general and about possible imitations in Jewish life. It was during this educational and political process that he came in close touch with Ha-Shomer Ha-Tzair people in the United States. The ideological and practical alliance he then forged with the radical kibbutz movement was thus ever imbued with a deep aversion toward Revisionism as a Jewish sort of fascism.[58]

Earlier in this essay, the strong animosity—ideological as well as personal—that Brandeis felt in 1919 toward Vladimir Jabotinsky, the world leader of the Revisionist movement, was referred to. Brandeis's antagonism and contempt even increased during the thirties. Beginning in 1933, Stephen Wise, expressing sentiments also shared by Brandeis, became an outspoken critic of Revisionism. He claimed the movement was essentially fascist and alien to the democratic spirit of Judaism and Zionism. Brandeis forcefully backed this anti-Revisionist course.[59]

Following the outbreak of World War II, Brandeis-Wise–inspired American Zionism acutely faced the challenge of the New Zionist Organization. Jabotinsky himself arrived in America in March 1940. He died suddenly later in that year; Revisionists in the United States, however, embarked on their own militant course from 1939-40. A leading sponsor of this trend was Ben Hecht, the famous novelist and playwright. It is most instructive to perceive how this advocate of Revisionism in America synthesized his Judaism with Americanism. Hecht's synthesis was dramatically the opposite of Brandeis's and helps, by comparison, to better understand not just the latter's sympathy for a group such as Avukah but also at the same time the essentials of Brandeisian Zionism. It is worthwhile to quote in some length from Ben Hecht's most interesting autobiography.

The German mass murder of the Jews, recently begun, had brought [in 1939] my Jewishness to the surface. I felt no grief or vicarious pain. I felt only a violence to-

ward the German killers, I saw the Germans as mur-
derers with red hands. Their fat necks and round,
boneless faces became the visages of beasts. Their de-
scent from humanity was as vivid in my eyes as if they
had grown four legs and a snout. . . .

The anger led me to join an organization for the first
time in my life. It was called "Fight for Freedom" and
was dedicated to bringing the U.S.A. into the war
against the Germans. . . .

I was aware that I was doing all these things as a Jew.
My eloquence in behalf of democracy was inspired
chiefly by my Jewish anger. I had been no partisan of
democracy in my earlier years. Its sins had seemed to
me more prominent than its virtues. But now that it was
the potential enemy of the new German Police State I
was its uncarping disciple. Thus, oddly, in addition to
becoming a Jew in 1939 I became also an American—
and remained one.[60]

For Hecht, then, American values were accidental to his
Zionism; and he adopted democracy once it became useful
for his Jewish interest. Brandeis's Zionism was precisely the
opposite. He conceptualized Zionism as deeply akin to the
American ethos; and he originally adopted Zionism once he
realized it could sustain and refine his Americanism. Brandeis
the Zionist of the thirties was far different from the one of
the teens; he would not talk now about taking Palestine "by
the way" to the Kingdom of Heaven. Still, he did retain his
belief that Jewish nationalism had to attest to the best of values
shared by Judaism and Americanism. The Revisionist movement, therefore, seemed to him anathema to all he cherished,
and he was fully disposed to support all kinds of democratic
groups firmly opposing that movement.

Of course, Brandeis sided with Avukah not just because
of its militant anti-Revisionist policies. He undoubtedly shared
the movement's compassionate commitment to the building
up of the Jewish homeland as a thoroughly progressive society. On the whole, though, there is no doubt that a good
part of Brandeis's support derived from nonpolitical sources.

He was attracted to idealistic and intelligent youth. And Avukah's connections with Ha-Shomer Ha-Tzair—as an educational and pioneering movement—also worked to nourish
Brandeis's attraction to the radical student organization.

All his Zionist life Brandeis was aligned with "general Zi-
onism," namely, the mainstream Zionist Organization of
America. Remembering his path to Judaism and Zionism via
American progressivism, it's not surprising that he often
leaned toward labor Zionism. In addition, Brandeis's mili-
tancy linked him to Zionist radical circles as well. Avukah and
Ha-Shomer Ha-Tzair thus appealed to Brandeis the militant
Progressive.

The Ha-Shomer Ha-Tzair kibbutz movement, however, appealed also to Brandeis the American Jew. Ein Ha-Shofet and
Ramat Ha-Shofet, pioneering settlements located on Palestine's Menasheh Hills, fully satisfied Brandeis's deep yearn-
ings for an ethnic identity. For him these kibbutzim not only
represented a social model of a City upon a Hill but also
offered him the happiness of sharing his brethren's good
fight.

In its last stage, Brandeis's Zionism became less conditional
upon the mission element. During this development Brandeis
synthesized his twin driving forces—contribution to the bet-
terment of society and belonging to a primordial group. He
also now identified with Zionism as a movement for assuring
the inalienable right of his people to live peacefully among
the nations. He perceived Zionism as a vital, creative movement carving out its own social patterns.

Still, Brandeis never embraced Zionism the way most European Zionists did. For them, Zionism was an organic movement, striving to bring about a total nationalist renaissance,
religious and historical traditions included. These latter elements remained absent from Brandeis's Zionism. Instead, he
emphasized the social and ethical values he believed were the
essence of Judaism. This belief served as the nexus binding
his Zionism with Americanism. Always a proud, idealistic
American, he conceptualized a deep kinship between Jewish
and American ideals. Zionism for him was ever bound to

achieve noble values—including freedom, justice, and the right of man to a dignified and creative life—that he considered common to the American promise and to the Jewish ethos.

---

1. Arthur Hertzberg, "Zionism, Ideological Evolution," *Encyclopedia Judaica* 16 (Jerusalem: Keter Publishing House, 1971): 1042-69.

2. Author's conclusions, based on research of Hadassah's and B'nai Brith's literary publications and educational programs, 1938-58.

3. Allon Gal, *Brandeis of Boston* (Cambridge, Mass: Harvard Univ. Press, 1980), especially chap. 4.

4. Ibid., especially chap. 5.

5. Ibid., 79-85, 169-81.

6. Melvin I. Urofsky, *American Zionism from Herzl to the Holocaust* (Garden City, N.Y.: Doubleday, 1975), chap. 4.

7. Gal, *Brandeis of Boston*, 147-62; Barbara A. Harris, "Zionist Speeches of Louis Dembitz Brandeis: A Critical Edition" (Ph.D. diss., University of California, L.A., 1967), 188-204, 491-504.

8. Gal, *Brandeis of Boston*, chap. 5; Harris, "Speeches," 96.

9. Allon Gal, "The Mission Motif in American Zionism (1898-1948)," *American Jewish History* 75 (June 1986): 363-85.

10. Allon Gal, "Brandeis's View on the Upbuilding of Palestine, 1914-1923," *Studies in Zionism* 6 (Autumn 1982): 216-22, 237-38; quot., ibid., 238.

11. Ibid., passim.

12. Cf. Ben Halpern, *A Clash of Heroes: Brandeis, Weizmann and American Zionism* (New York: Oxford Univ. Press, 1987), chap. 5.

13. Gal, "Brandeis's View," 216.

14. Joseph B. Schechtman, *The Vladimir Jabotinsky Story*, 2 vols. (New York: Thomas Yoseloff, 1956-61), 1:320-21.

15. Cf., Halpern, *Clash of Heroes*, chap. 3.

16. Brandeis to Ahad Ha'am, Sept. 3, 1917, Jewish and National University Library, Jerusalem, Private Archives, J-10-6.

17. Brandeis to Ahad Ha'am, Nov. 4, 1918, ibid. In this letter Brandeis wrote in continuation, "Through your pupil, Alfred Zimmern, and otherwise, your lessons in Jewish nationalism are receiving ever wide application and influence." In Brandeis's eyes, Sir Zimmern, an English political scientist, authority on foreign affairs, and author of *The Greek Commonwealth* (1911), was considered a pupil

of Ahad Ha'am. This amazing assumption of Brandeis did fit though to his peculiar concept of Zionism; for him both Zimmern and Ahad Ha'am were pursuing a general moral legacy he thought was the essence of Zionism; cf., Philippa Strum, *Louis D. Brandeis: Justice for the People* (Cambridge, Mass.: Harvard Univ. Press, 1984), 237-43.

18. Harris, "Speeches," 139, 143-45.

19. Ibid., 100.

20. Yonathan Shapiro, *Leadership of the American Zionist Organization, 1897-1930* (Urbana: Univ. of Illinois Press, 1971), especially chap. 9.

21. Melvin I. Urofsky, *A Voice That Spoke for Justice: The Life and Times of Stephen S. Wise* (Albany: State Univ. of New York Press, 1982), 263-69; quot., ibid., 264.

22. Ibid., 263-69.

23. Brandeis to Robert Szold, Aug. 19, 1930, in Melvin I. Urofsky and David W. Levy, eds., *The Letters of Louis D. Brandeis*, 5 vols. (Albany: State Univ. of New York Press, 1971-), 5:447 (abbreviated hereafter as BL).

24. Halpern, *Clash of Heroes*, chap. 6; contributions to self-defense, e.g., Brandeis to Szold, Oct. 5, 1936; March 4, 1937 ("for disposition as Ben-Gurion may direct"), BL, 5:582, 586, respectively.

25. Brandeis to Frankfurter, Sept. 20, 1929, BL 5:386.

26. The author's interview with Paul A. Freund (law clerk to Brandeis, 1932-33; later Harvard professor), Cambridge, Mass., Nov., 1973.

27. Halpern, *Clash of Heroes*, chap. 6.

28. Ibid.

29. Gal, *Brandeis of Boston*, 76-77, 102; Brandeis to Mack, Jan. 29, 1930, BL, 5:416; and ed. note 1, ibid., 417.

30. Brandeis to Szold, Aug. 19, 1930, BL, 5:447.

31. Quot., ibid.

32. Ibid., letters and ed. notes, 416ff.

33. Allon Gal, *David Ben-Gurion—Preparing for a Jewish State* (Sede Boqer Campus, 1985) [Hebrew], to be published in English by the Jewish Publication Society, Philadelphia, chaps. 2-6, and passim. Ben-Gurion to Brandeis, Jan. 5, 1934, and Brandeis to Ben-Gurion, Jan. 25, 1934, BL, 5:531-33; Brandeis to Stephen S. Wise, June 2, 1936, BL, 5:571.

34. Gal, *David Ben-Gurion*, chaps. 2-6.

35. See n. 38, below. For a detailed account of Brandeis's relations with labor Zionism, see Allon Gal, "Brandeis' Social-Zionism," *Studies in Zionism* 8 (forthcoming).

36. Brandeis to Frankfurter, Feb. 26, 1927, *BL*, 5:272-73.

37. Gal, *Brandeis of Boston*, 120-21; Brandeis to Josephine Gold-mark, Jan. 8, Oct. 30, 1932, and to Morris L. Ernst, Dec. 24, 1936, BL, 5:492, 512, 585, respectively.

38. Harry Viteles, *History of the Cooperative Movement in Israel*, 7 vols. (London: Vallentine, Mitchell, 1966-70). Vol. 1 dwells mainly on the evolution of the cooperative movement in the pre-Israel years.

39. Urofsky, *American Zionism*, 250-57; quot., Brandeis to Szold, Aug. 19, 1930, BL, 5:448; for support see, e.g., Brandeis's letters during Aug.-Nov. 1930, BL, 5:446-66.

40. Elkana Margalit, *"Hashomer Hatzair"—From Youth Community to Revolutionary Marxism* (Tel-Aviv: Hakibbutz Hameuchad Publishing House, 1971) [Hebrew], introduction, conclusion, and passim.

41. Irma L. Lindheim, *Parallel Quest: A Search of a Person and a People* (New York: Thomas Yoseloff, 1962), 320-21.

42. Shmuel Ben-Zvi to the author, Jan. 30, 1987; see also his "Justice Brandeis and Ein Hashofet," *New Palestine* 22, no. 4 (Nov. 14, 1941): 10-12. "Address by Mordecai Bentov of Mishmar Haemek at Brandeis Memorial Meeting, Ein Hashofet, Oct. 16, 1941," Ein Ha-Shofet Archives. (I am indebted to Shmuel Ben-Zvi for his contribution for and assistance in the exploration of the Brandeis/Ha-Shomer Ha-Tzair theme.)

43. Bentov to Brandeis, Feb. 24, 1933, Ein Ha-Shofet Archives.

44. Bentov to Brandeis, May 30, 1934, Ein Ha-Shofet Archives.

45. Ibid.

46. Ibid.; and see n. 14, above.

47. Ibid.; Bentov to Brandeis, May 30, 1934, Ein Ha-Shofet Archives.

48. N. 42, above; Leibner/Brandeis correspondence, Aug. 1936-June 1940, Ein Ha-Shofet Archives; letters, memoirs, and articles by Ben-Zvi, Bentov, Lindheim, Leibner, and others in Shmuel Ben-Zvi., ed., *Joshua Leibner* (Kibbutz Ein Ha-Shofet & Ha-Shomer Ha-Tzair Organization, 1957) [Hebrew], especially 4-73. Background, Shmuel Dothan, *Partition of Eretz-Israel in Mandatory Period* (Jerusalem: Defense Ministry Publishing House, 1979) [Hebrew], chaps. 2, 4, 5.

49. N. 42 above; Ben-Zvi/Brandeis correspondence, March-July 1941, Ein Ha-Shofet Archives; Shmuel Ben-Zvi, "Brandeis and Ein Ha-Shofet," Ein Ha-Shofet Archives.

50. Quot., Brandeis to Szold, May 10, 1939, BL, 5:618; Ramat Ha-Shofet, *Ramat Ha-Shofet's 25th Year Anniversary* (Ramat Ha-Shofet: Kibbutz Ramat Ha-Shofet, 1966) [Hebrew], 58-59. (I am thankful to Eliezer Rabinovitz of Ramat Ha-Shofet Archives for his cooperation.)

51. Brandeis/Szold correspondence related to Palestine Endowment Funds, Sept.-Oct. 1938, Brandeis Univ. Archives, Brandeis Col-

lection, Box 12; "Disbursements of Louis D. Brandeis Fund for 1940," Zionist Archives and Library, R. Szold Collection IX/7; and n. 42.

52. Margalit, *"Hashomer Hatzair,"* chap. 7; Susan L. Hattis, *The Bi-National Idea in Palestine during Mandatory Times* (Tel-Aviv: Shikmona Publishing, 1970), 71-73, 229-55.

53. Lindheim in her eulogy of J. Leibner, in Ben-Zvi, *Leibner,* 7; Philip S. Bernstein, "My Pilgrimages to Brandeis," *Reconstructionist* 7, no. 17 (Dec. 26, 1941): 9-11; quot., ibid., 11.

54. Mordecai S. Chertoff, "Avukah," *Encyclopedia of Zionism and Israel,* 2 vols. (New York: Herzl Press/McGraw-Hill, 1971), 1:99; radicalization, *Avukah Student Action* 1, no. 1 (Sept. 23, 1938), 4, no. 1 (Oct. 31, 1941), New York Public Library, Jewish Collection. (I am grateful to Seymour Melman for his cooperation.) Avukah's pamphlets at the Zionist Archives and Library; the author interviews with Ben Halpern (with Avukah 1930-36, with He-Chalutz 1936 on; later professor at Brandeis University), Brookline, Mass., Oct. 1986; Nathan Glazer (with Avukah 1941-42, later Harvard professor), New York City, Jan. 1987; Zellig Harris, New York City, Nov. 1986, March 1987; Seymour Melman (with Avukah 1935-41), New York City, Jan. 1987.

55. Editorial, "We Take Our Stand," in *Avukah Student Action* 1, no. 1 (Sept. 23, 1938): 1-2; 1941, 1942 conventions' resolutions, Zionist Archives and Library; quot., Avukah, *Program for American Jews* (New York City: Avukah, 1938, rev. 1941), 10-11. [Twelve-page pamphlet at the Zionist Archives and Library].

56. Nn. 54, 55, above.

57. Brandeis/Szold correspondence related to Palestine Endowment Funds, 1938-41, Brandeis Univ. Archives, L. Brandeis Collection, Box 12, and Zionist Archives and Library, R. Szold Collection, IX/31; interviews with Harris; quot., Brandeis to Wise, Nov. 1, 1936, ibid., X/14; reports of Harris in letters to Brandeis, e.g., June 20, 1939, Jan. 13, Aug. 18, 1941, ibid., X/31.

58. Author's interview with Zellig Harris, New York City, March 1987; and see n. 54 above.

59. Brandeis to Wise, March 19, 1935, BL, 5:551.

60. Ben Hecht, *A Child of the Century* (New York: Simon & Schuster, 1954), 517-18.

Brandeis and the
Progressive Movement

DAVID W. LEVY

The purpose of this essay, as is obvious from its title, is to bring into relationship a man and a movement. How complete a Progressive *was* Louis Dembitz Brandeis? Where precisely did he "fit" into that movement? To what extent did the movement echo his ideas and predispositions? To what extent did its achievements satisfy his hopes and its failures dash them? The assumption, of course, is that in the process of ruminating about the relationship, both the individual and the movement may be more clearly understood.

The central problem in such an undertaking will at once be obvious to any historian and to any intelligent nonhistorian who reflects upon the matter for even a moment. Brandeis was a single individual, after all; and although, like other men, he was capable of complexity and open to change, he is probably more notable for his steadiness, his consistency, his having, as Professors Paul Freund and Melvin Urofsky have both argued, an essentially unified and unfragmented mind.[1] We know, by now, a great deal about him: what positions he espoused, what he believed in, what he loved and hated. It seems fairly safe to predict that additional information about Brandeis will probably not lead to upsetting and entirely unpredictable revelations. The picture of him in our scholarship is clear, growing clearer, and not likely to be overturned.[2]

It can never be the same in the case of movements. There may have been a time in our historiography when it was sufficiently revealing to point out that William Lloyd Garrison was "an abolitionist" or that Samuel Adams was "a revolutionary." But with our growing understanding of social movements, our growing appreciation of how complicated and shifting all such social alliances really are, this extrapolation from some movement to a substantial delineation of an individual who was a part of it is no longer possible. We now find it necessary to ask what *kind* of an abolitionist was Garrison, what *sort* of a revolutionary was Adams, what *manner* of a progressive was Louis D. Brandeis? And if this trick of fitting individuals into some larger movement is difficult for any such collection of diverse persons, it is especially hard in the case of the Progressive movement.

That social alliance was composed of men and women who had arrived at their progressivism by traveling along a bewildering variety of routes. Some of them came through the agrarian protest of the late nineteenth century. Others made their journeys through social work, through the labor movement, through politics, socialism, or the Single Tax movement of Henry George. Many were drawn by certain shocking experiences in various urban settings; some by their commitments to American Protestantism. There were numerous journalists, academics, attorneys, and businessmen. And given this tremendous diversity of career and experience among progressive reformers, it will not be surprising that they came with different agendas, different political allegiances, different priorities and programs, different diagnoses of the evils that troubled America, different prescriptions for restoring the nation to good health. Nor should it be surprising that the prescriptions of some of them conflicted with the prescriptions of others.

There is no need to rehearse here the details of their debates—over what to do about the trusts, over prohibition, over women's suffrage and immigration restriction, over labor unions and conservation and a half-dozen other matters. Some who thought of themselves as progressives looked forward boldly to a new America of fresh opportunities and opening possibilities; others looked backward nostalgically to a simpler, more decent and neighborly society. Some put their faith in the people and worked for more democracy; others were betting on organized labor or a new political party or a company of social scientists, technicians, and other experts. Some thought that present evils could be cured and a better society ushered in by ending the corrupt practices in business and politics; others advocated far-reaching structural changes in government. Because it was subject to such internal tensions and strains, to such heated debates over fundamental policies among individuals who undoubtedly thought of themselves as members of the same embattled company, progressivism has eluded, far more than most movements in our history, precise definition.[3]

"The more that historians learn," Peter Filene concluded in a famous article of 1970, "the farther they move from consensus." Filene, in fact, was so impressed by the swirling diversity and disagreement within progressivism that he rejected the whole notion of there having been "a movement" at all.[4] Historical scholarship since Filene's 1970 verdict has not taken so extreme a position. Through the seventies and eighties, historians of the period have tried to recognize the diversity within progressivism while continuing to insist that there really was, at the heart of the activity, some common core that was sufficient to define a movement after all. Many of these historians have tried to make sense of the movement by dividing progressives into subgroups or factions within the larger ferment.[5] Others—arguing that even these broad factions cannot properly encompass the diversity within progressivism or pointing out that too many progressives partook of beliefs and advocated courses of action that wandered easily across the factional boundaries—have tried to suggest other grounds for the existence of a Progressive movement. Some have resorted to listing certain underlying principles that united the movement, principles that were general enough to sanction the diversity or vague enough in their terminology (appeals to "the people" or to "efficiency" or to "honest government") to cloak disagreements over concrete courses of action.[6] Other historians have contended that, for now, the most promising approach to understanding progressivism is to abandon the search for some "essence" and to concentrate instead upon the particular elements of its appeal, the lineage of its various aspects, the individual careers of its practitioners, the ways in which its fluctuating coalitions came together and broke apart.

After the last two decades of spirited debate, therefore, it seems clear that historians will continue to emphasize the diversity of progressivism, continue to insist that, despite this diversity, a genuine social movement of considerable importance did in fact exist, and continue to search for whatever unifying principles they can discover. In that pursuit they will inevitably turn frequently to the reforming career of one of the central figures of the era, Louis D. Brandeis. Where, in this confusion of experience, analysis, presupposition, and program, did the Boston attorney belong?

It is clear that he had very little to do with a great many facets of the Progressive movement. We do not see him engaged in the attempt to bring about world peace, for example. Nor does he seem to care much about the settlement-house movement or about social work in general. He is not involved in wiping out prostitution or in attempts to improve the public health. He is not a worker for progressive education or for improving the family or for bettering conditions for prisoners. We do not find him trying to abolish child labor or to improve urban housing or to ameliorate the condition of black Americans. And yet some of these causes worked improvements in the lives of millions of American citizens, and all of them can be considered as parts of the Progressive movement.

Brandeis's interests were confined almost entirely to political and economic reform. He came to progressivism, moreover, out of a profound unease and anxiety about the modern world and out of a resulting wish to restore to this country some of the characteristics and habits of an earlier and happier time. He belonged to the party of nostalgia, and he carried in his makeup a picture, perhaps mythical, of a past America that was more upright, simple, and congenial. His progressivism was born out of an attempt to restore that America by combating the most troubling and intrusive of modern evils.

That Brandeis was *temperamentally* ill at ease with many of the innovations of the modern world is perfectly clear. He

avoided telephones whenever he possibly could. He hated
the automobile and much preferred to walk. (In 1927 he con-
gratulated his daughter for the "thrilling news" that his
grandson was learning to walk. "It's fortunate he is learning
now. By the time he reaches maturity the art may be among
the lost—through disuse."[7]) For those occasions when the
grandfather himself could not walk, he kept his horse and
buggy until he was forced off the streets of Washington, D.C.,
in the mid-twenties. Modern advertising was, to him, a per-
nicious vice, and he complained about it for all of his mature
life. The modern obsession with fashion repulsed him. "We
are living in an artificial age, and artificiality is ruining many
of those just starting out in life. . . . The little struggling clerk
must bedeck his wife with bizarre clothes so he can take her
out and impress upon those who behold her in all her mag-
nificence that he is making big money."[8]

Above all, it was this ostentation, this obsession with luxury, the high and soft living of the rich (and, even worse, of
those who tried to appear rich) that appalled and depressed
him. H.L. Mencken remembered that, as a lad who hated
exercise himself, he was always profoundly surprised when
he encountered an athletic boy who "showed a capacity for
articulate speech."[9] In the same way, Brandeis often seemed
slightly surprised when he encountered someone raised under the habits of modern luxury who turned out to be public-
spirited, honest, and high-minded. One of his best friends
was a businessman and playboy named Herbert White, whose
main talent seemed to be befriending the rich and powerful.
"Herbert is quite his old good self," Brandeis reported to his
brother Alfred. "Not visibly affected by his rich associations
(& no riches himself). . . . Herbert was South with [James J.]
Storrow this winter—a part of the time at a small rich-man's
club in No. Carolina (60,000 acres) and then visiting a friend
in South Carolina (30,000). Lucullus was ein Hund dagegen
[a dog by comparison]. Father would have said: 'Nichts er-
freuhliches [not very pleasant].' It is evident, you & I are relics
of a past world—which I prefer."[10]

His own vacations were almost always flights from urban
civilization and modern conveniences—off to Dedham,

Maine, the Canadian woods, or Cape Cod. He preferred dignified, old hotels to modern, luxurious ones. In 1914 he wrote to Alfred from one of the latter sort in Detroit: "At this hotel, I was introduced to the modernist stunt of having not only an orchestra at dinner and singers, but also dancers. Pompeii and Alexandria are being emulated. I guess a heavy batch of adversity wouldn't hurt American morals."[11] In 1926 the Brandeises abandoned the Washington apartment where they had lived for more than a decade. "The 'improvements,' " the justice wrote Julian Mack, "have at last driven us from Stoneleigh."[12] His furniture was strong and simple ("buy nothing your grandchildren cannot use," he once advised[13]).

This distaste for much of what was new in America was at the heart of his character, and many who commented upon him—particularly in his old age—remarked upon the simplicity of his life-style, his austerity, his hatred of luxury, his spare diet. That was the meaning, probably, of the many observers who compared him to an Old Testament prophet and who thought of him that way. His personal habits and preferences seemed like a righteous rebuke to the stupidities, the complexities, the frills of the twentieth century.

This temperament made itself felt in his progressivism as well as in his way of life. He looked back over American history (like many other Progressives who hailed from the West, from rural regions, and from small business backgrounds and found themselves in places like Chicago, New York, or Boston) and detected a falling away from old virtues, the introduction into American life of harmful and dangerous tendencies. And he set out to apply his tremendous energies, his luminous intelligence, and his legal and political skills in an effort to oppose them.

Brandeis was particularly distressed by three things that, he believed, had newly entered our national life and that were in danger of spoiling it: first, the corruption of American society—the threat to the country caused by an excessive devotion to materialism and personal greed and the resultant evaporation of the old republican virtues of community service, honesty, and public honor; second, the growth of enmities and tensions between the industrial classes and the consequent breakdown of the sense of mutual respect and community feeling that, he thought, had characterized an earlier America; and third, the rapid consolidation of American business and American government that had taken place during the last years of the nineteenth and the first years of the twentieth centuries.

Probably the first thing that attracted his attention and that set his feet down the road to progressivism was the discovery of substantial corruption in business, in government, and in the relations between them.[14] Professor Allon Gal recounts the story of Brandeis, at age ten, accusing the treasurer of a Louisville debating society of loose accounting—the scoundrel could not properly account for forty cents.[15] He supported Grover Cleveland in 1884 largely because he thought James G. Blaine was dishonest. And his earliest work in Boston reform circles was with the Civil Service Reform Association, the Boston Citizenship Committee, the Massachusetts Society for Promoting Good Citizenship, and the Election Laws League. He was one of the moving spirits behind the Good Government Association.[16]

The story of Brandeis and William Ellis, his client, is well known. Ellis was a liquor dealer, and in 1890 Brandeis called him into his office, handed him a list of Massachusetts state legislators, and asked him which could be bribed. Ellis calmly checked the names off. Brandeis said, "Ellis, do you realize what you are doing?" and discoursed upon the evils of bribery until the tears ran down his client's face.[17] It was his hatred of corrupt lobbying and legislative practices that led him to the battle against the Boston Elevated Railway Company and to the formation of the Public Franchise League after 1897. Brandeis's speech to the Boot and Shoe Club in March 1903 was his fullest statement on municipal corruption, bribery, and the unwholesome relationship between businessmen and politicians. His solution was a simple one (so simple, in fact, as to open him to the charge that at this stage of his reforming career he was still unsophisticated, naive, and simplistic): "It is needed that public opinion be aroused, and that good, honest, honorable men be drafted into service as our office holders."[18]

Brandeis never outgrew his outrage at dishonesty in high places. The Pinchot-Ballinger conservation controversy of 1910, for example, that great crusade against Taft's Department of the Interior for selling reserved land to the Guggenheim interests, the public battle that first lifted Brandeis to national attention, will be misunderstood if it is seen as being principally about the conservation of natural resources. Principally, it was about public officials who had not honestly discharged their duties and who had thereby betrayed the people of the United States.[19] And Brandeis's bitter comments on the accounting methods of the Lipsky Zionists in the twenties[20] or on the culprits in the Teapot Dome scandals[21] show that the boy who wanted to know what had become of the forty cents never lost his passion for honesty in the discharge of the public business or his insistence that corrupt men be replaced by honest ones.

Even more distressing to Brandeis than the discovery of new levels of public corruption among modern businessmen and politicians was a second intrusion into the new industrial society, an intrusion even more disturbing and dangerous. He thought that he was able to fix an exact date to this new realization on his part. In 1891 he had been asked to teach a course on business law at the Massachusetts Institute of Technology. While he was dutifully preparing his lectures, news came of the bloody suppression of the Homestead strike in Pennsylvania. His own description of what happened is a fine account of its impact on his own views and of the extent to which he saw the trouble as a genuine intrusion of a modern evil upon a healthier and more peaceful America.

I think it was the affair at Homestead which first set me to thinking seriously about the labor problem. It took the shock of that battle, where organized capital hired a private army to shoot at organized labor for resisting an arbitrary cut in wages, to turn my mind definitely toward a searching study of the relations of labor to industry.

I had been asked to give a course on Business Law at the Massachusetts Institute of Technology, and had gone to some pains to prepare my lectures, tracing the evolution of the common law in its relation to industry and commerce, when one morning the newspaper carried the story of the pitched battle between the Pinkertons on the barge and the barricaded steel workers on the bank. I saw at once that the common law, built up under simpler conditions of living, gave an inadequate basis for the adjustments of the complex relations of the modern factory system. I threw away my notes and approached my theme from new angles. Those talks at Tech marked an epoch in my own career.[22]

The realization that industrial classes were approaching dangerously near to a state of war led Brandeis to take an important role in that sort of progressivism that concerned itself with industrial conditions. His work in this field can be considered under two heads: efforts to reach accommodation and understanding between the capitalists and the workers and efforts to improve the condition of the workers.

In a 1904 speech, delivered before a group of employers who had just been engaged in a bitter strike, Brandeis laid down the principles of "industrial democracy." "Some way must be worked out by which employers and employees, each recognizing the proper sphere of the other, will each be free to work for their own and for the common good, and that the powers of the individual employee may be developed to the utmost. To attain that end, it is essential that neither should feel that he stands in the power—at the mercy—of the other." For their part, employers must recognize at once and without hesitation the right of workers to organize; for their part, workers must behave responsibly and legally in the conduct of their affairs.[23]

Brandeis's work on behalf of better understanding between capital and labor absorbed him for thousands of hours in the first decade of the twentieth century. That work ranged from

efforts to persuade businessmen, like his clients E.A. Filene
and William H. McElwain, to institute various forms of "industrial democracy," to personal arbitration of management-
labor disputes under the auspices of the National Civic
Federation, to spirited advocacy of various schemes designed
to ensure regularity of employment for the benefit of both
workers and owners.[24] No doubt his best known attempt to
bring peace between warring industrial classes was in the
famous New York garment strike of 1910. By winning the
confidence of both sides in this gigantic strike and by prompt-
ing both sides to see the advantages each had in arbitration
and cooperation (as well as by endless patience, stunning
diplomatic skill, and high imagination), Brandeis was able to
achieve a "Protocol of Peace" that restored some order to that
chaotic industry—at least for a time.[25]

It should be noted that in his role as bringer of peace to
the new industrial classes, he was not, by any means, always
on the side of the workers. He debated no less a labor-hero
than Samuel Gompers, president of the AFL, for example,
taking the position that labor unions should be incorporated
and thereby held accountable for their acts.[26] He fearlessly
evangelized for *scientific management*, a term he invented himself, despite the fears and resentments of his labor allies, who
saw the invasion of efficiency experts as a threat to fair labor
conditions.[27] And when he believed that railroad owners
were entitled to higher rates, he was willing to take their part
although it was not a popular position as far as consumers,
shippers, and workers were concerned.[28]

But most often Brandeis was, in fact, to be found on the
side of the workers. In 1906 he began his lifelong effort to
provide affordable life insurance to Massachusetts workers
through the state's system of savings banks. It was that reform, he later said, that gave him the most satisfaction of any
he ever undertook; and the reason for it was nothing less than
to free Massachusetts workers from their bondage to the commercial life insurance companies and to provide them with
that financial security without which they could never hope
to be free men and women.[29] He also gave attention to bettering pension plans for workers and to combating discre-

tionary pensions that he regarded as a new kind of peonage.[30] Finally, Brandeis used his talents as a lawyer to defend before various state courts and before the Supreme Court progressive laws designed to regulate the hours and wages of American workers.[31]

Louis Brandeis is no doubt best remembered as a progressive, however, for his battles against the third dangerous intrusion into modern American life—what he called "the curse of bigness." The industrial giants, created by new techniques of management, helped along by questionable and often illegal practices, were, for Brandeis, the great enemies of traditional American democracy. He had always been a foe of monopoly, of course, and one of his earliest public fights, back in the 1880s, had been against the monopoly held by the Boston Disinfecting Company.[32] But by 1910 the battle against big business domination had become the central tenet of his progressivism. His dogged, ten-year struggle against the attempts of the New York, New Haven, and Hartford Railroad to acquire a monopoly over New England transportation, his testimony before numberless congressional committees, his book, *Other People's Money and How the Bankers Use It*, the frontal attack on the "money trust"—all indicate the ferocity of his opposition to bigness in the economic sphere.

Before he was finished, he tried to connect bigness to all of the other evils he and other progressive spokesmen had detected. Bigness was the real source of the corruption of our political life; bigness was the real cause of waste and inefficiency (the claims of the advocates of large units of production notwithstanding); bigness was at the heart of the disrespect for law in modern America; bigness was responsible for the rape of our natural resources; bigness poisoned democracy at its very source—the belief in the rough equality of the American people. Bigness treated its employees the worst. And its intrusion into American economic life threatened that spirit of adventure, invention, and initiative that accounted for so much that was good about the national character.[33] By the time Brandeis was appointed to the Supreme Court in 1916, he was no doubt best known in the country at large as the

chief opponent of monopoly and the man who was advising
President Wilson about how to destroy this evil, restore competition, and return America to that condition of relative economic equality and small-unit production that had existed
before this serpent entered into the American garden.

It is worth noting that recent criticisms of Brandeis as a
progressive reformer have focused on this very characteristic,
his single-minded attempt to turn back the clock by combating
the invasion of big business. Historians who have considered
his reform career have almost universally given Brandeis high
marks for his integrity of purpose, his tactical sense and or-
ganizational skill, his courage and inventiveness. Those who
have criticized him, however, have concentrated their fire on
two aspects of his battle against the curse of bigness. First,
they have argued that his stubborn insistence that his economic proposals were uniquely moral and that, therefore, the
positions of his foes were based entirely on selfishness and
disregard of the public good was blind and unfair. In fact,
these historians insist, Brandeis's opponents were often simply men possessed by an alternate—and more modern—view
of the economic needs of American society. And second, some
historians have argued that Brandeis's economic thought was
so hopelessly wedded to small-unit production and the destruction of bigness that he badly misunderstood the forces
underlying American economic life and consistently advocated shortsighted and counterproductive policies.[34]

Brandeis's hatred of bigness included a hatred of big government, as is well known. The thrust of his advice to Wilson
in the campaign of 1912 was that monopoly could be controlled without (as Theodore Roosevelt seemed to be arguing)
erecting a huge government bureaucracy to manage the
process.[35] Thus, Brandeis was a firm believer and an active
champion of the rights of states and localities to conduct ven-
turesome social experiments and to develop distinctive local
culture. (His generous and meticulous interest in the University of Louisville must be seen in the context of this desire
that American economic, social, and cultural life be decentralized.[36]) He insisted that states had to resist encroaching
federal authority if they wished to preserve their integrity and

the liberty of their citizenry. Brandeis opposed centralized government for the same reasons that he opposed consolidated business—it was bound to be inefficient, it was bound to be too powerful to accommodate itself to the democratic process, it was bound to be open to corruption and careless and brutal in the use of its tremendous power.

This, in brief, was Brandeis's kind of progressivism. He was deeply disturbed by recent trends in American life because he thought they were endangering the nation he knew. The explosion of heavy industry seemed to carry with it unlimited possibilities for blind materialism, political corruption of the worst sort, class warfare and hatred, quite unacceptable limitations on human freedom, the death of initiative and healthy competition, the gravest threat to traditional standards of democracy itself. For him, therefore, progressivism meant the rolling back of dangerous economic and political intruders. In part, no doubt, he was led to this analysis—serpents of evil entering into the garden of American happiness—by his Kentucky boyhood, by his temperament, by the small-businessmen clients he attracted and served so well and for so long. But in part, it must be acknowledged, he was led into this posture of opposition by an extremely thorough study of American business practices, by a set of very high standards for human behavior, and by a relentless and fearless conscience.

Before closing this discussion, it seems appropriate to suggest, very briefly, two additional points—in order to redeem the assertion, at the beginning, that putting "Brandeis" and "progressivism" into relationship might help to illuminate both the individual and the movement. Thus, one point has to do with him and one with progressivism.

It must not be assumed that simply because Brandeis took his bearings by some vision of the American past that he was closed to innovative and experimental measures. His experiments, it is true, were directed toward the restoration of an older and better time, but he was a bold and inventive reformer. He took a little known English device, the "sliding-scale," and applied it to the Boston gas situation—by his plan, adopted in 1906, dividends to stockholders were tied directly to reductions in the price of gas charged to consumers.[37] Savings Bank Life Insurance was his idea from start to finish. The "preferential union shop" was his way of breaking the deadlock between management and labor in the garment strike.[38] This flexibility enabled him to join hands with other progressives in establishing the Federal Trade Commission, the Federal Reserve System, the Clayton Antitrust Act, and other measures during the Wilson administration.[39]

And what is to be learned about the Progressive movement from this analysis of Brandeis's place in it? Simply that it was always a chaotic and unplanned mingling of men and ideas, of shifting coalitions and differing perspectives—chaotic, but able to agree enough and come together enough and compromise enough to accomplish a wide variety of significant and important reforms. As Daniel Levine wrote in 1964, "Federal regulation of corporations may appear to one man as a method of protecting a rural way of life, to another as encouraging small businessmen, to still another as promoting social justice for factory workers, to a fourth as asserting federal responsibility for national economic health, to a fifth as forestalling more radical measures."[40] The central fact to remember about Brandeis as a progressive is not that his own private vision led him into tension with other reformers who were each moved by their own private visions. The central point is about how many views they held in common, how well they were able to cooperate on certain ends (even though moved by differing outlooks), how many particular measures they were able to endorse and work for, shoulder to shoulder.

Louis Dembitz Brandeis was a part of this jumbled effort of rival purposes and temporary alliances, of divergent visions and personal agendas that combined to form the Progressive movement. Because of his reputation, his stature, his age (a little older than the other leading reformers), and because of his wide range of acquaintanceship within the movement, he was a very important part of it all.[41] He had his private views, of course, and he held them strongly. But in his integrity of purpose, his relative freedom from doctrinaire solutions (if not from a doctrinaire insistence on his diagnosis of the curse of bigness), and his readiness to work with others—even those who approached the problems of America in different ways—he represented what was best about the Progressive movement, and it is entirely fitting that he should be remembered as one of its most effective and important representatives.

---

1. For this theme, see Paul A. Freund, "Mr. Justice Brandeis: A Centennial Memoir," 70 *Harvard Law Review* 769 (1956); and Melvin I. Urofsky, *A Mind of One Piece: Brandeis and American Reform* (New York: Scribner's, 1971).

2. The standard biography is Alpheus T. Mason, *Brandeis: A Free Man's Life* (New York: Viking Press, 1956). Recent scholarship has added much to our understanding of Brandeis's life and thought, however, and readers are referred particularly to the following works published during the eighties: Allon Gal, *Brandeis of Boston* (Cambridge, Mass.: Harvard Univ. Press, 1980); Nelson L. Dawson, *Louis D. Brandeis, Felix Frankfurter, and the New Deal* (Hamden, Conn.: Archon Books, 1980); Melvin I. Urofsky, *Louis D. Brandeis and the Progressive Tradition* (Boston: Little, Brown, 1981); Bruce Allen Murphy, *The Brandeis/Frankfurter Connection: The Secret Political Activities of Two Supreme Court Justices* (New York: Oxford Univ. Press, 1982); Lewis J. Paper, *Brandeis* (Englewood Cliffs, N.J.: Prentice-Hall, 1983); Philippa Strum, *Louis D. Brandeis: Justice for the People* (Cambridge, Mass.: Harvard Univ. Press, 1984); and Thomas K. McCraw, "Louis D. Brandeis Reappraised," *American Scholar* 54 (1985): 525-36.

3. For challenging and perceptive newer studies that underline and demonstrate the wide variety within the Progressive movement, see Richard Hofstadter, *The Age of Reform* (New York: Vintage Books, 1955); David W. Noble, *The Paradox of Progressive Thought* (Minneapolis: Univ. of Minnesota Press, 1958); Charles Forcey, *The Crossroads of Liberalism: Croly, Weyl, Lippmann and the Progressive Era* (New York: Oxford Univ. Press, 1961); Christopher Lasch, *The New Radicalism in America, 1889-1963: The Intellectual as a Social Type* (New York: Vintage Books, 1965); Gabriel Kolko, *The Triumph of Conservatism* (New York: Free Press, 1963); Robert Wiebe, *The Search for Order, 1877-1920* (New York: Hill & Wang, 1967); Jean B. Quandt, *From the Small Town to the Great Community: The Social Thought of Progressive*

Intellectuals (New Brunswick, N.J.: Rutgers Univ. Press, 1970); David P. Thelen, *The New Citizenship: Origins of Progressivism in Wisconsin, 1885-1900* (Columbia: Univ. of Missouri Press, 1972); James B. Gilbert, *Designing the Industrial State: The Intellectual Pursuit of Collectivism in America, 1880-1940* (Chicago: Quadrangle Books, 1972); John D. Buenker, *Urban Liberalism and Progressive Reform* (New York: Scribner's, 1973); Lewis L. Gould, ed., *The Progressive Era* (Syracuse: Syracuse Univ. Press, 1974); John D. Buenker, John C. Burnham, and Robert M. Crunden, *Progressivism* (Cambridge, Mass.: Schenkman, 1977); Aileen Kraditor, *The Radical Persuasion, 1890-1917* (Baton Rouge: Louisiana State Univ. Press, 1981); Robert M. Crunden, *Ministers of Reform: The Progressives' Achievement in American Civilization, 1889-1920* (New York: Basic Books, 1982); Dewey W. Grantham, *Southern Progressivism: The Reconciliation of Progress and Tradition* (Knoxville: Univ. of Tennessee Press, 1983); James T. Kloppenberg, *Uncertain Victory: Social Democracy and Progressivism in European and American Thought, 1870-1920* (New York: Oxford Univ. Press, 1986); and David B. Danbom, *"The World of Hope": Progressives and the Struggle for an Ethical Public Life* (Philadelphia: Temple Univ. Press, 1987). For three helpful guides through this welter of interpretation, see David M. Kennedy, "Progressivism: An Overview," *Historian* 37 (1975): 453-68; Richard L. McCormick, "The Discovery That Business Corrupts Politics: A Reappraisal of the Origins of Progressivism, *American Historical Review* 86 (1981): 247-74; and Daniel T. Rodgers, "In Search of Progressivism," *Reviews in American History* 10 (1982): 113-32.

4. Peter G. Filene, "An Obituary for the Progressive Movement," *American Quarterly* 22 (1970): 20-34.

5. The split over the "trust issue" in the election of 1912 was so visible and so widely commented upon that historians have always recognized that particular division. For a pioneering attempt to note the factionalization within progressivism in broader terms, see John Braeman, "Seven Progressives," *Business History Review* 35 (1961): 581-92. For an able discussion of recent efforts to make sense out of the Progressive movement by breaking it up into factions, see Rodgers, "In Search of Progressivism."

6. For an entirely reasonable recent attempt, see Richard L. McCormick, "Progressivism: A Contemporary Reassessment," in his *The Party Period and Public Policy: American Politics from the Age of Jackson to the Progressive Era* (New York: Oxford Univ. Press, 1986), 263-88, especially 269-73.

7. Brandeis to Susan Brandeis Gilbert, Oct. 16, 1927, Susan Brandeis Gilbert Mss., Brandeis University.

8. From an interview, "Mr. Brandeis on the Cost of Living," *New York Herald Tribune*, March 3, 1912; quoted in Mason, *Brandeis*, 423-24. For some comments on advertising, see letters to H.W. Ashley, Jan. 31, 1914; to Felix Frankfurter, Sept. 30, 1922; to George H. Soule, April 22, 1923, in Melvin I. Urofsky and David W. Levy, eds., *The Letters of Louis D. Brandeis*, 5 vols. (Albany: State Univ. of New York Press, 1971–), 3:239 and 5:70, 92 (abbreviated hereafter as BL). For his attitude toward automobiles, see Paper, *Brandeis*, 1.

9. H.L. Mencken, "Adventures of a Y.M.C.A. Lad," in his *Heathen Days, 1890-1936* (New York: A.A. Knopf, 1943), 30.

10. Brandeis to Alfred Brandeis, March 28, 1926, BL, 5:214.

11. Brandeis to Alfred Brandeis, Oct. 16, 1914, BL, 3:330-31.

12. Brandeis to Julian W. Mack, Sept. 3, 1926, Julian W. Mack Mss., Zionist Archives, New York City.

13. Brandeis to the Brandeis family, winter 1880-81, BL, 1:60.

14. For an indication that Brandeis's coming to progressivism on the basis of this perception was typical of many other Progressives, see McCormick, "The Discovery That Business Corrupts Politics."

15. Gal, *Brandeis of Boston*, 22.

16. Ibid., 22-23.

17. Mason, *Brandeis*, 89-90.

18. The speech is reprinted as "Address on Corruption," in Osmond K. Fraenkel, ed., *The Curse of Bigness: Miscellaneous Papers of Louis D. Brandeis* (New York: Viking Press, 1934), 263-65. For Brandeis's work against municipal corruption with the Public Franchise League, see Mason, *Brandeis*, chaps. 7-9; Paper, *Brandeis*, chaps. 5-6; Strum, *Brandeis*, chap. 5.

19. For Brandeis's role in the Pinchot-Ballinger controversy, see Mason, *Brandeis*, chap. 17; Paper, *Brandeis*, chap. 9; and Strum, *Brandeis*, 132-40.

20. See, for example, Brandeis to Felix Frankfurter, Oct. 21, 1920, to Julian W. Mack, Nov. 17, 1920, and to Mack, July 5, 1928, BL, 4:490 and 506, 5:347. See also, Melvin I. Urofsky, *American Zionism from Herzl to the Holocaust* (Garden City, N.Y.: Anchor, Doubleday, 1975), chap. 7 and 346-57.

21. Brandeis's bitter comments on the Teapot Dome scandals and the corrupt practices they revealed can be found in numerous letters to Felix Frankfurter. See especially letters of March 8, 17, 1924, and March 4, 1928, BL, 5:120, 122, and 327.

22. Mason, *Brandeis*, 87-88; Strum, *Brandeis*, 95-96.

23. Brandeis's speech before the Boston Typothetae was published as "The Employer and the Trades Unions." See Brandeis,

Business—A Profession (Boston: Small, Maynard & Co., 1914), 13-27.

24. For this aspect of Brandeis's work, see Mason, *Brandeis*, chap. 10; and Strum, *Brandeis*, chap. 7. See also the title address in Brandeis, *Business—A Profession*, 1-12. For an early example of his lifelong devotion to securing regularity of employment, see his long letter to A. Lincoln Filene, June 1911, BL, 2:444.

25. See Mason, *Brandeis*, chap. 19; Paper, *Brandeis*, chap. 10; or Strum, *Brandeis*, 174-79.

26. Brandeis's side of the debate against Gompers (Dec. 4, 1901) was published as "The Incorporation of Trades Unions," in Brandeis, *Business—A Profession*, 88-98.

27. For Brandeis's role in the "efficiency movement," see Mason, *Brandeis*, 323-33; Paper, *Brandeis*, 151-54; or Strum, *Brandeis*, 160-69. See also, Samuel Haber, *Efficiency and Uplift: Scientific Management and the Progressive Era, 1890-1920* (Chicago: Univ. of Chicago Press, 1964).

28. Brandeis's work in the Railroad Rate case hearings is described in Mason, *Brandeis*, chaps. 20-21; and Paper, *Brandeis*, chap. 11.

29. The struggle for Savings Bank Life Insurance is recounted most thoroughly in Alpheus T. Mason, *The Brandeis Way: A Case Study in the Workings of Democracy* (Princeton: Princeton Univ. Press, 1938). For briefer accounts, see Mason, *Brandeis*, chap. 11; Paper, *Brandeis*, chap. 7; or Strum, *Brandeis*, chap. 6.

30. Louis D. Brandeis, "Our New Peonage: Discretionary Pensions," *Independent* 72 (July 25, 1912): 187-91; reprinted in idem, *Business—A Profession*, 71-87.

31. For Brandeis's part in defending social legislation in the courts, see Mason, *Brandeis*, chap. 16; Paper, *Brandeis*, chap. 12; or Strum, *Brandeis*, chap. 8.

32. Paper, *Brandeis*, 55; Strum, *Brandeis*, 55.

33. Indictment of the curse of bigness is a constant and omnipresent theme in Brandeis's thought from about 1908 onward. For examples, see Brandeis, *Other People's Money and How the Bankers Use It* (New York: F.A. Stokes & Co., 1914); the middle entries in his *Business—A Profession*, 205-328; and Fraenkel, *Curse of Bigness*, Part III. The evil of bigness was also consistently hit upon when Brandeis testified before various congressional committees between 1911 and 1916; for references to this body of testimony, see Fraenkel, *Curse of Bigness*, 180-81.

34. This line of criticism began in a path-breaking article, Richard

M. Abrams, "Brandeis and the New Haven–Boston & Maine Merger Battle Revisited," *Business History Review* 36 (1962): 408-30. A more hostile attack is Albro Martin, *Enterprise Denied: Origins of the Decline of American Railroads, 1897-1917* (New York: Columbia Univ. Press, 1971). The critique of Brandeis's economic views is handled most responsibly and intelligently, however, in the Pulitzer Prize–winning book, Thomas K. McCraw, *Prophets of Regulation: Charles Francis Adams, Louis D. Brandeis, James M. Landis, Alfred E. Kahn* (Cambridge, Mass.: Harvard Univ. Press, 1984), chaps. 3-4. McCraw's criticisms can also be found in his "Louis D. Brandeis Reappraised."

35. On this point, see John Milton Cooper, Jr., *The Warrior and the Priest: Woodrow Wilson and Theodore Roosevelt* (Cambridge, Mass.: Harvard Univ. Press, 1983).

36. Bernard Flexner, *Justice Brandeis and the University of Louisville* (Louisville: Univ. of Louisville, 1938).

37. Brandeis, "How Boston Solved the Gas Problem," *American Review of Reviews* 26 (Nov. 1906): 594-98; reprinted in idem, *Business— A Profession*, 99-114. See also, Mason, *Brandeis*, chap. 9; Paper, *Brandeis*, chap. 6; or Strum *Brandeis*, 67-72.

38. The "preferential union shop" was defined by Brandeis as "providing that the manufacturers should, in the employment of labor hereafter, give preference to union men, where the union men are equal in efficiency to any non-union applicants." For the garment strike, see the references in n. 25, above.

39. For Brandeis's role as one of the architects of President Wilson's "New Freedom" legislation, see Mason, *Brandeis*, chap. 26; Strum, *Brandeis*, 209-16, 221-23; and McCraw, *Prophets of Regulation*, chap. 4. See also, Arthur S. Link, *Wilson: The New Freedom* (Princeton: Princeton Univ. Press, 1956), 212, 423-38.

40. Daniel Levine, *Varieties of Reform Thought* (Madison: State Historical Society of Wisconsin, 1964), xi.

41. This idea of Brandeis's important role within the movement as a whole is developed in Melvin I. Urofsky, "Linchpin of Reform," in idem, *A Mind of One Piece*, chap. 7.

Brandeis and the Living Constitution

PHILIPPA STRUM

The conference at which this paper was delivered was entitled "A Mind of One Piece,"[1] a phrase used by Felix Frankfurter to describe Brandeis's complete and cohesive political and judicial philosophy (and, later, the title of Melvin Urofsky's impressive book about Brandeis). Brandeis's former law clerk and friend Paul Freund has written that "it is hardly likely that anyone came to the Supreme Court with a more closely articulated set of convictions than those which Brandeis held."[2] Brandeis did indeed develop his beliefs before he reached the Court. They did not change after he became a justice, but, as Professor Mary K. Tachau stated, the convictions he took to the Court changed the Constitution for all time. One of the things he did was to emphasize its nature as a *living* constitution, and it is to that topic that I should like to address myself.

In order to do so, I propose to discuss Brandeis's view of human nature, his view of law, his closely allied view of constitutional interpretation, and, finally, his great importance to the civil liberties and particularly the freedom of speech that we enjoy today.

Brandeis declared to Harold Laski that human beings are "wee things," and he wrote in one of his major decisions, "Man is weak and his judgment is at best fallible."[3] But for Brandeis, the infinite fallibility of human beings was balanced by their infinite educability. That ability to learn is one of the keys to Brandeis's philosophy and his perception of human nature.

Because human beings are fallible, their endeavors, whether economic or political, must be kept small. And so he believed in democracy, which he saw as the active participation in any institutional entity—political, economic, social—of all the people involved in it, so that no one person attempted or was expected to play a role more extensive than that manageable by any single human being.

Alvin Johnson once called Brandeis an "implacable democrat." Dean Acheson labeled him an "incurable optimist."[4] He was both, believing that sufficient doses of democracy inevitably result in a good political system. He emphasized the need of human beings for the leisure during which to fulfill their possibilities for individual creativity. His ultimate goal, therefore, was liberty. Everything else in his thinking followed from that. The role of the state, the Supreme Court included, was to create the circumstances that would enable people to fulfill their potential. This meant maximizing their liberty—whether by protecting their access to ideas or by protecting them from economic forces that would encroach upon their liberty to create—by giving them adequate wages, adequate leisure, and an adequate opportunity to participate in the economic decision-making process.

Brandeis's starting point was the human being, with his and her capabilities and limitations. Another element in his thought, and one that illuminated his view of the law, is what is now known as sociological jurisprudence. At the Harvard Law School, where he studied the case method introduced by Prof. Christopher Langdell, he learned that it is frequently cases that establish principles of law. Langdell declared: "Law . . . consists of certain principles or doctrines. . . . Each of these doctrines has arrived at its present state by slow degrees [through a series of cases]. . . . To have such a mastery of these as to be able to apply them with constant facility and certainty to the ever-tangled skein of human affairs, is what constitutes a true lawyer."[5] Law, therefore, cannot be understood as a fixed entity but rather as something that moves, changes, and undergoes transformation. Statutes represent solutions to factual problems that have arisen at particular historical moments, so to understand statutes, it is necessary to understand their historical underpinnings. Law is reflective of current social facts, of present felt necessities, and of the legal response to them considered most appropriate. The role of the constitutional lawyer, in the legal system perceived through the prism of sociological jurisprudence, is to present the judge with the larger social facts behind the particular felt necessity that resulted in a law and the connection between the necessity and the law. The role of the judge, it follows logically, is to learn from the lawyers. (Or so Brandeis believed when he was a practicing attorney; he carved out a more active role for judges when he himself became one.)

The Brandeis brief, the first brief that had more pages by far of statistics than of legal principles, was, of course, seminal. It exemplified the method of explaining to a court the facts that make a law reasonable and, therefore, bring it within the purview of the Constitution. One of the facts of which Brandeis was well aware was that the major work on the brief had been done by his sister-in-law, Josephine Goldmark; and consequently, he wanted to give her credit by taking the highly unusual step of putting on the front page of the brief the name not only of a woman but of a nonlawyer. He felt, however, that the United States Supreme Court was not ready for either but promised to put her name on the next brief they produced together. He did, citing her as his "assistant" on the title page of their next major brief.[6]

The vision of the Constitution embodied in that brief and in Brandeis's thinking was one that combined permanence and change, as the basic law of the land must do. It creates institutional and procedural imperatives, such as federalism, separation of powers, and responsiveness to the people. The last implies the existence both of change and of limitations on the power of governmental institutions. The Supreme Court was one of the institutions so affected, and Brandeis viewed the Constitution as giving the Court a very limited mandate. In a democracy social policy is made by legislatures, not by judges, and the Constitution must be read as requiring the Court to exercise judicial restraint. Brandeis laid down the basic rules of constitutional adjudication. Judges must not render an opinion in the absence of a real conflict, as when parties seeking to overturn a law agree to sue each other. Judges must not hear a case when the matter involved is not ripe for decision. Whenever possible, judges must decide on statutory rather than on constitutional grounds. Supreme Court justices must not decide the meaning of local and state laws but accept the interpretation of the highest court of the state. Judges must consider the consequences of their decisions. If, for example, a particular decision would imply creation of a new right, judges must be aware of all possible ramifications. When the Court was asked to validate a property right in news dispatches, it was Brandeis who refused to go along on the grounds that the ultimate consequence would be the end of freedom of ideas. And most important of all, Brandeis urged judges to interpret both the Constitution and the cases before them on the narrowest possible grounds. The net result was an enjoinder to judges to limit their input.[7]

The logical consequences of Brandeisian judicial restraint were the handing down of opinions upholding constitutional laws Brandeis disliked or declaring unconstitutional laws he considered to embody desirable social policy but to be beyond the constitutional powers of those who enacted them. Above all, he supported the right of state legislatures to experiment and the duty of the Supreme Court to uphold the constitutionality of their experiments. Very much the federalist, Brandeis was opposed to centralization of power. This was part of his dislike and fear of bigness, which he felt would simply get out of hand. While he nonetheless supported the doctrine that the Constitution permits creation of the kind of federal police power embodied in the Wagner Act, the Fair Labor Standards Act, and the Social Security Act, he opposed both turning amorphous areas of power over to federal officials and the tendency of the federal government to become overly big by assuming powers that more properly belonged to the states. Along with Lord Acton, Brandeis believed that power tends to corrupt and that absolute power corrupts absolutely. Therefore, he voted against both the unilateral power of the president to fire executive officials when a statute required Senate agreement and the vast powers given to the president by the National Industrial Recovery Act. He explained his attitude toward New Deal decisions in this way. "I have not been against increase of federal power, but curtailment of State's powers."[8]

The most important contribution of Brandeis to constitutional interpretation and to keeping the Constitution a living one was his emphasis on facts. Justice Oliver Wendell Holmes and others such as Roscoe Pound were among the first to recognize that laws changed and indeed ought to change in response to the felt necessities of the people. But neither Holmes nor Pound told judges how to ascertain what the felt necessities of the people were, so that the judges would know what alterations in constitutional interpretation were justified by changing societal circumstances.

Sociologist David Riesman, who clerked for Brandeis and left the law in part because he felt unable to live up to the standard set by him, wrote that Holmes's opinions "merely told how not to interpret the Constitution," whereas Brandeis "has tried . . . to lay the ground work of a pattern of constitutional interpretation." That was indeed Brandeis's self-assigned task. He interpreted sociological jurisprudence as meaning that judges had a duty to take judicial notice of facts, and he urged them to do independent fact-gathering before rendering judgment. In one of his more famous decisions, he declared that the reasonableness of state regulations "can ordinarily be determined only by a consideration of the contemporary conditions, social, industrial and political, of the community to be affected thereby. Resort to such facts is necessary, among other things, in order to appreciate the evils sought to be remedied and the possible effects of the remedy proposed."[9]

But appreciation of the evils that legislatures sought to overcome did not imply the desirability of automatic acceptance by the Court of any and all state legislation. Brandeis had spent most of his adult life in Massachusetts and had fought for much of that time against the corruption that ran rampant through the halls of the State House. He was scarcely ready to accept a state legislature's judgment of rationality—that, in fact, was why judges had to do their own fact-finding—but he was ready to bend over backward to allow the states to experiment with remedies for problems he considered to be real.

Perhaps his best statement of this approach was in the case of *Jay Burns Baking Company* v. *Bryan*, which involved a statute regulating the size of loaves of bread sold in Nebraska. Brandeis's opinion included fifteen pages of information about the baking industry, most of it in footnotes. It is with some amusement that one remembers that it was to a bench of Supreme Court justices, not a meeting of either baking industry representatives or social scientists, that Brandeis said he and his brethren "had merely to acquaint ourselves with the art of breadmaking and the usages of the trade; with the devices by which buyers of bread are imposed upon and honest bakers or dealers are subjected by their dishonest fellows to unfair competition; with the problems which have confronted public officials charged with the enforcement of the laws prohibiting short weights, and with their experience in administering those laws."[10]

Occasionally, his emphasis on giving states as much leeway as was defensible led Brandeis to differ with his fellow sociological jurisprudent, Oliver Wendell Holmes. *Pennsylvania Coal* v. *Mahon* involved a Pennsylvania act that forbade mining of anthracite coal in a manner that would cause the subsidence of a home. A coal company that retained mining rights under land on which a home was subsequently built and was then prohibited by the statute from exercising its rights sued, charging that the act violated the due process clause of the Fourteenth Amendment. Holmes, writing for the Court, agreed that the state had taken property without compensation after having contracted to give the mining rights to the company. Brandeis stated in dissent that state protection of individual safety was a legitimate concern and that the law was a reasonable way of achieving it. Brandeis summed up what he considered to be the two justices' differences of approach when he told Frankfurter that "Holmes did not advocate [state experimentation]; he put up with it."[11] Even when the two men came out on the same side, it was frequently for different reasons. *Truax* v. *Corrigan* permitted state injunctions against picketing. Brandeis used fourteen pages to cite other state laws, concluding that the injunction was not an unreasonable way for the legislature to deal with the problem of labor picketing. Holmes took a relatively laconic two pages to find such injunctions not prohibited by the Fourteenth Amendment.[12] The "originator" of sociological jurisprudence made a purely legal argument; Brandeis looked at the facts.

The result of Brandeis's emphasis on facts was that his law clerks found themselves spending far more time in the Library of Congress than in the law library. They had to tell Brandeis what was happening in the "real world." Brandeis's opinions contain citations of studies, statistics, censuses; this was what he meant by a democratic judiciary's being responsive to the people and their needs. He wanted to know what nonjudges thought. When Felix Frankfurter and James Landis began work on their *Business of the United States Supreme Court* and asked Brandeis what made the Court such a good one, Brandeis replied that one element was "the play of public opinion upon the Court's performance." As a young man, he had helped create the *Harvard Law Review*. While on the bench he became the first justice to use extensive citations of law review articles, with which he made himself familiar so as to know what lawyers not in contact with the Court were thinking. Magazines of opinion and newspapers were equally important.[13]

There was one area in which there was very little room for change as far as Justice Brandeis was concerned, and that was the First Amendment's guarantee of free speech and press. In this, he went much further than did Holmes.

Brandeis hated the Fourteenth Amendment because the Court had turned it into a vehicle for the striking down of experimental economic legislation being enacted by various states. He felt that if it had to remain in existence, the amendment should be used only to ensure that state legislatures observed procedural regularities and to protect those things "fundamental" to a democratic system. These he listed as "Right to Speech. Right to Education. Right to choice of profession. "Right to locomotion."[14] In *Pierce* v. *United States*, Brandeis argued that free speech was needed to safeguard

the "fundamental right of free men to strive for better conditions through new legislation and new institutions."[15]
Speech came first, but notice that education came second. It,
like speech, could be limited only in the rarest of circumstances, because without education there would be no free flow
of ideas; without education the members of democracy would
not have access to the ideas they needed in order to be able
to vote intelligently.

This was true at *all* times. Holmes's famous "clear and
present danger" doctrine holds that government can restrict
speech more stringently in time of war than in time of peace.
Brandeis gradually came to disagree, and his disagreement
has received too little attention. Brandeis dissented in *Shaefer*
v. *United States*, a 1920 case that was typical of the somewhat
hysterical prosecutions for sedition during World War I. After
asserting erroneously that "the constitutional right of free
speech has been declared to be the same in peace and in war,"
Brandeis went on to enunciate his own principle. "In peace
too men may differ widely as to what loyalty our country
demands and an intolerant majority swayed by passion or by
fear may be prone in the future as it has often been in the
past to stamp as disloyal opinions with which it disagrees."
He added that he found it acceptable for government to leg-
islate against espionage (although only during wartime) but
not against sedition. Sedition is no more than ideas of which
the government disapproves; the important point is that it *is*
ideas and so must be permitted.[16]

Brandeis's comment about the right of speech being the
same in peacetime and in wartime was more than wishful
thinking (the Court in fact had never made such a declaration);
it represented his recognition that speech is never as necessary as it is during war, when people are being asked to make
the supreme sacrifice for their country. Neither was he convinced that the sanctity of property or the fear of violence was
sufficient to stifle speech. In the soaring paean to speech that
constitutes his concurrence in *Whitney* v. *California*, he declared that even the likelihood that speech will result in "some
violence or in destruction of property is not enough to justify
its suppression. There must be the probability of serious in-

jury to the State." Note that he spoke of the "probability," not the possibility, of "serious injury" to the state. There must be imminent danger of the overthrow of the state before speech can be suppressed. Obviously, he was not advocating waiting until people were actually marching into government buildings carrying bombs, but neither was he convinced that a few students demonstrating on a campus and perhaps doing some property damage was sufficient reason to stop them. On the contrary, he would no doubt have approved campus activism as part of one's education in democracy, for he believed a politically inactive electorate to be the "greatest danger to freedom."[17] And that is where Holmes and Brandeis disagreed.

In 1920 the Court upheld the Minnesota law prohibiting anything, including speech, that would interfere with military enlistment. Holmes concurred; Brandeis dissented, saying that Congress had preempted the field for such laws under the war power and that in any event the speech being punished (attacking conscription because it had not been voted upon by the general electorate) was harmless.[18]

Holmes has traditionally been considered more of a philosopher, Brandeis a pragmatist. It is therefore instructive to realize that it was Brandeis who looked deeply into the political philosophy that underlies the Constitution and found a much greater need to protect speech and the free flow of ideas than did Holmes. One reason for the difference between them was that Brandeis saw speech not only as an end but as a means. Brandeis believed in absolute truth; among his absolute truths were beliefs in human limitations, human educability, the corrupting nature of power, the evils of bigness, and the importance of individual dignity. Holmes, however, saw democracy—as opposed to Social Darwinism—as embodying no absolute truths and therefore could not see speech as an end in and of itself. His famous reference to the "marketplace of ideas" was extremely utilitarian, as was his statement that "I am so skeptical as to our knowledge about the goodness and badness of laws that I have no practical criterion except what the crowd wants." Brandeis couldn't have said that. *He* could recognize the difference between good and bad laws as well as between good and bad ideas. Their disagreement lay in the implication of Holmes's position that the Constitution doesn't give the Court the positive obligation to protect the free speech of the people, as opposed to the negative duty to prevent government from interfering with speech unnecessarily.[19]

A discussion of Brandeis's constitutionalism necessarily includes the right that he had made famous long before he joined the Court: the right to be left alone, or privacy. Brandeis and his partner Samuel Warren's article, "The Right to Privacy," which appeared in the 1890 *Harvard Law Review,* was the first American law review discussion of that key right. And although the genesis of the article was the intrusive press coverage that followed Warren's engagement to a member of another prominent Boston family, the argument in it went far beyond media reporting of private matters.[20]

The article claimed that all human beings are entitled to a certain amount of isolation and that public scrutiny, in a situation deserving of privacy, constitutes an assault on dignity. It was, of course, intrusion by the press that was Brandeis's and Warren's immediate concern.

But Brandeis considered intrusions upon privacy by the government even more serious because they endangered democracy. Privacy—whether of the individual or of the group—is necessary to the creation, development, and communication of ideas. His concurrence in *Whitney* included the statement: "Those who won our independence believed that the final end of the State was to make men free to develop their faculties. . . . They believed freedom to think as you will and to speak as you think are means indispensable to the discovery and spread of political truth." Speech has value in a democratic political system only if it follows or encourages thought. Added to Brandeis's insistence that "public discussion is a political duty," this means that the privacy vital to thought is a constitutional necessity, implicit in the First Amendment.[21]

It is implicit in the Third, Fourth, Fifth, and Ninth amendments as well, and Brandeis emphasized its importance to the Fourth Amendment in his dissent in the case of *Olmstead* v.

United States. Outraged by a criminal conviction based on wiretapping, Brandeis proclaimed: "The makers of our Constitution undertook . . . to protect Americans in their beliefs, their thoughts, their emotions, and their sensations. They conferred, as against the Government, the right to be let alone—the most comprehensive of rights and the right most valued by civilized men. To protect that right, every unjustifiable intrusion upon the privacy of the individual, whatever the means employed, must be deemed a violation of the Fourth Amendment."[22]

For someone who emphasized speech and education as consistently as did Brandeis, it is telling that he called privacy, rather than speech or education, "the right most valued by civilized men." Clearly, he assumed that both free speech and education were dependent upon privacy, which is one of the reasons that privacy was labeled "the most comprehensive of rights." It protects people in their isolation, in their homes, in their workplaces, in their interchanges with other people. The man who said that "if we would guide by the light of reason, we must let our minds be bold" knew that bold minds would not remain so if government deprived them of the privacy to consider, play with, discard, adopt, and refine ideas, either by themselves or in concert with others. He was unhappy that "discovery and invention have made it possible for the Government, by means far more effective than stretching upon the rack, to obtain disclosure in court of what is whispered in the closet. . . . The progress of science in furnishing the Government with means of espionage is not likely to stop with wire tapping. Ways may some day be developed by which the Government, without removing papers from secret drawers, can reproduce them in court, and by which it will be enabled to expose to a jury the most intimate occurrences of the home." Brandeis asked, in horror, "Can it be that the Constitution affords no protection against such invasions of individual security?" It is worth noting that Brandeis's working folder in the *Olmstead* case contains a 1928 newspaper clipping, reporting on the development of something called television. Clearly, technology held perils for privacy and for democracy as well.[23]

Brandeis believed in a dynamic, changing constitution. His was a constitutional philosophy diametrically opposed to that of *original intent*, if that term signifies treating the Constitution as a fossil rather than as a living entity. What would he say were he to hear the late twentieth-century version of an unchanging constitution, especially in the manifestation rejecting privacy as a constitutional right? His comments about some of his colleagues less eager than he to legitimize constitutional experimentation and judicial protection of individual rights are suggestive. Brandeis described his colleague Mahlon Pitney as "much influenced by his experience and he has had mighty little." He thought Pierce Butler "has given no sign of anything except a thoroughly mediocre mind." And he despaired of Justice Joseph McKenna, "The only way of dealing with him is to appoint guardians for him."[24]

He also said, as was noted above, "If we would guide by the light of reason, we must let our minds be bold." It is neither reasonable nor bold to assume that the writers of the Constitution, who were both, meant their document to be permanently ossified in the society of 1787. Brandeis's constitutionalism was reasonable and bold, and it ensures him a prominent place in that small pantheon of thinkers who could see both our faults and our potential and, falling prey to neither despair nor complacency, utilize them as the building blocks for a mode of judicial interpretation appropriate to both a democratic political system and a changing Constitution.[25]

----

1. Every Brandeis scholar owes his or her thanks to the wonderful people in the University of Louisville Archives who have been so generous with their help and who, I suspect, know more about Brandeis than any of the rest of us. Thanks are also due to many of the other Brandeis scholars, because I discovered while writing about Brandeis that others similarly engaged were willing to share their material. That is sufficiently unusual in the academic world to warrant notice. And so for his help, I would like to thank in particular Mel Urofsky, who, in addition to providing encouragement and suggestions, has, along with David Levy, been so important to our work and that of others by making the Brandeis letters available beyond

the walls of the Archives and the other collections in which they are to be found. (Melvin I. Urofsky and David W. Levy, eds., *The Letters of Louis D. Brandeis,* 5 vols. [Albany: State Univ. of New York Press, 1971–] [abbreviated hereafter as BL]).

2. Felix Frankfurter, "Mr. Justice Brandeis and the Constitution," 43 *Harvard Law Review* 33 (1931): 104; Melvin I. Urofsky, *A Mind of One Piece* (New York: Scribner's, 1971); Paul Freund, *On Understanding the Supreme Court* (Boston: Little, Brown, 1949), 52.

3. *New State Ice Company* v. *Liebmann,* 284 U.S. 262 (1932) (dissenting), 310.

4. Alvin Johnson to Brandeis, quoted in Alexander M. Bickel, *The Unpublished Opinions of Mr. Justice Brandeis* (Cambridge, Mass.: Harvard Univ. Press, 1957), 163; Dean Acheson, *Morning and Noon* (Boston: Houghton Mifflin, 1965), 102.

5. Christopher Columbus Langdell, *Selected Cases on Contracts* (Boston: Little, Brown, 1871), quoted in Louis D. Brandeis, "The Harvard Law School," *Green Bag,* Jan. 1889, 19-20.

6. The Brandeis brief was first used in the case of *Muller* v. *Oregon,* 208 U.S. 412 (1908). Brandeis wanting to use Goldmark's name: Philippa Strum, *Louis D. Brandeis: Justice for the People* (Cambridge, Mass.: Harvard Univ. Press, 1984), 123, citing Josephine C. Goldmark, *Impatient Crusader: Florence Kelly's Life Story* (Urbana: Univ. of Illinois Press, 1953), 158-64. The brief in which she was named was submitted in *People* v. *Eldering,* 254 Ill. 579 (1912).

7. The most complete statement of the rules Brandeis wished the justices to set for themselves is found in his opinion in *Ashwander* v. *Tennessee Valley Authority,* 275 U.S. 288 (1936), 341-48. Cf., Brandeis to Frankfurter, Sept. 19, 1922, BL, 5:64. Creation of property right in news dispatches: *International News Service* v. *Associated Press,* 248 U.S. 215 (1918) (dissenting), 248, 262-63, 267.

8. Cases in which he voted to uphold laws with which he disagreed or to strike down laws of which he otherwise approved as beyond the constitutional powers of those enacting them: see, e.g., *New State Ice; Yarborough* v. *Yarborough,* 290 U.S. 202 (1933); additional cases discussed in Strum, *Brandeis,* 302-7; Bickel, *Unpublished Opinions,* 5-19. On experimentation by states: *New State Ice,* 306-11; *Liggett* v. *Lee,* 288 U.S. 517 (1933) (dissenting), 522, 548-49, 568-69. On bigness: Osmond K. Fraenkel, ed., *The Curse of Bigness: Miscellaneous Papers of Louis D. Brandeis* (New York: Viking Press, 1934); Strum, *Brandeis,* 349-52. Federal police power: Nelson L. Dawson, *Louis D. Brandeis, Felix Frankfurter, and the New Deal* (Hamden, Conn.: Archon Books, 1980), 28-33, 101-23; Strum, *Brandeis,* 348-49. Presidential

power to fire officials: *Myers* v. *United States*, 272 U.S. 52 (1927) (dissenting), 250-93. NIRA: *Schechter* v. *United States*, 295 U.S. 495 (1935). Attitude: Quoted by Frankfurter in "Memorandum," Felix Frankfurter Papers, Library of Congress, Box 128, p. 24 (abbreviated hereafter as FP).

9. Author's interview with Prof. David Riesman, Dec. 4, 1977; David Riesman, "Notes for an Essay on Justice Brandeis," May 22, 1936, FP, Box 127, pp. 1-2. See continuation of Riesman memo in Strum, *Brandeis*, 311. On considering facts: *Truax* v. *Corrigan*, 257 U.S. 312 (1921) (dissenting), 355. For additional discussion of the differences in Brandeis's and Holmes's use of facts, see Urofsky, *Mind of One Piece*, 133, 146; Strum, *Brandeis*, 307-14.

10. *Jay Burns Baking Company* v. *Bryan*, 264 U.S. 504 (1924) (dissenting), 519-34.

11. *Pennsylvania Coal Company* v. *Mahon*, 260 U.S. 393, 415, 416 (1922). Brandeis's dissent: 260 U.S. 416, 422. Brandeis on Holmes and experimentation: Frankfurter, "Memorandum," FP, Box 124, p. 24.

12. *Truax*, 344, 354, 357-570. Holmes's statements about sociological jurisprudence run through his opinions, as do Brandeis's. The major theoretical statement by Holmes on the subject is Oliver Wendell Holmes, Jr., *The Common Law* (Boston: Little, Brown, 1881), especially Lecture I. Also see the essays and addresses published in idem, *Collected Legal Papers* (New York: Harcourt, Brace, 1921). Among Pound's many works, see especially Roscoe Pound, *The Spirit of the Common Law* (Boston: Marshall Jones, 1921); and idem, *An Introduction to the Philosophy of Law* (New Haven: Yale Univ. Press, 1922). Also see writings listed in George A. Strait, *A Bibliography of the Writings of Roscoe Pound* (Cambridge, Mass.: Harvard Law School Library, 1960).

13. Clerks's research: Strum, *Brandeis*, 355-57. Brandeis to Frankfurter, June 5, 1927, BL, 5:292-93. Brandeis's thoughts about the Supreme Court are printed in their entirety in Felix Frankfurter and James M. Landis, *The Business of the Supreme Court* (New York: Macmillan, 1928), vii-viii. *Harvard Law Review:* Alpheus T. Mason, *Brandeis: A Free Man's Life* (New York: Viking Press, 1946), 67. Citations of law review articles and other publications: Strum, *Brandeis*, 304, 342, 363-64. Brandeis first cited law review articles in *Adams* v. *Tanner*, 244 U.S. 590 (1917) (dissenting), 597, 603 n. 3, 613 nn. 1-3, 615 n. 1.

14. Quoted in Felix Frankfurter, "Memorandum," FP, Harvard Law School, 114-8, p. 19.

15. *Pierce* v. *United States*, 252, U.S. 239 (1920) (dissenting), 256.

16. Holmes in *Schenck* v. *United States*, 249 U.S. 47 (1919), 52; Brandeis in *Shaefer* v. *United States*, 251 U.S. 266 (1920) (dissenting), 495.

17. *Whitney* v. *California*, 274 U.S. 357 (1927) (concurring), 377-78, 375.

18. *Gilbert* v. *Minnesota*, 254 U.S. 325 (1920). Holmes's concurrence is at 334. Brandeis's dissent is at 325-43.

19. On the differences between Brandeis and Holmes concerning civil liberties: Samuel J. Konefsky, *The Legacy of Holmes and Brandeis: A Study in the Influence of Ideas* (New York: Macmillan, 1956), chaps. 9-10; Strum, *Brandeis*, 314-22, 335; Urofsky, *Mind of One Piece*, 141-47. The "marketplace of ideas" reference is part of Holmes's dissent in *Abrams* v. *United States*, 250 U.S. 616 (1919). The exact words are "the ultimate good desired is better reached by free trade in ideas. . . . the best test of truth is the power of the thought to get itself accepted in the competition of the market." Holmes's comment on knowledge: Mark DeWolfe Howe, *The Holmes-Pollock Letters* (Cambridge, Mass.: Harvard Univ. Press, 1941), 1:163.

20. Louis D. Brandeis and Samuel D. Warren, Jr., "The Right to Privacy," 4 *Harvard Law Review* 193-220 (1890-91).

21. *Whitney*, 377, 375.

22. *Olmstead* v. *United States*, 277 U.S. 438 (1928) (dissenting), 478.

23. "minds be bold": *New State Ice*, 311. Wiretapping: *Olmstead*, 474, 477. *Olmstead* folder: Brandeis Papers, Harvard Law School, 48-7.

24. On Justices Pitney, Butler, and McKenna: Felix Frankfurter, "Memorandum," FP, Box 224, pp. 17, 25, 26.

25. *New State Ice*, 311.

The Brandeis Agenda

MELVIN I. UROFSKY

A little over twenty years ago, I drove down to Louisville, Kentucky, to work in the Louis D. Brandeis Papers for the first time. My dissertation topic had just been approved by the history faculty at Columbia, and I was eager to begin research on the relationship between Brandeis and Woodrow Wilson to test Arthur S. Link's description of Brandeis as "the intellectual architect of the New Freedom."[1] As it turned out, there was not enough in the manuscripts to support a doctoral thesis,[2] but the wealth of material I found in the papers convinced me to find some other area in which to use them.

Little did I guess at the time that the bulk of my research activity for the next two decades would, either directly or indirectly, be tied to the life and career of one man. That initial trip led me to join with David W. Levy in editing the Brandeis Letters,[3] to various essays and articles on Brandeis as well as an interpretive biography,[4] to extensive research on American Zionism,[5] and to further work on two of Brandeis's chief lieutenants, Stephen S. Wise and Felix Frankfurter.[6] I became involved for a time in American Zionist affairs and tried to restate the Brandeisian philosophy, an endeavor that failed to succeed in the seventies as it had in the conflict between American and European Zionists six decades earlier.[7] Brandeis's influence relit a smoldering interest in the law, so that at age forty I entered law school and, like him, found the study of law a great delight as well as an enormously satisfying intellectual challenge.

But things have changed a great deal since 1965. I am older and, I hope, a little wiser, although my enthusiasm for the subject remains intense. More important are the vast changes in the field of Brandeisian scholarship. When David Levy and I published the first volume of the *Letters* in 1971, we expressed the hope that it might lead other scholars to reexamine various aspects of his career.[8] While we would certainly not claim that renewed interest in Brandeis stems solely from our work, we do know that many writers have utilized the *Letters* extensively, and they have been in touch with us over questions raised in their research. Needless to say, we have derived much satisfaction from this.

It is not my intention to review all of the scholarly literature on Brandeis. Rather, I would like to suggest an explanation for this torrent of writing and why some of it often appears so argumentative. Then I want to offer some suggestions for research to be done, the "Brandeis agenda," if you will, in the next twenty years.

In 1965 nearly all of the material available on Louis Brandeis reflected the awe and devotion he had inspired in two generations of reformers.[9] Early biographers such as Jacob de Haas[10] and Alfred Lief[11] were embarrassing in their adulation. Alpheus T. Mason's semiauthorized *Brandeis: A Free Man's Life* appeared in 1946 and culminated over a decade of monographic studies on particular aspects of Brandeis's career.[12] Mason was the first to have access to Brandeis's nonjudicial papers and also interviewed the justice several times after Brandeis had retired from the bench. Yet although Mason raised one or two questions about Brandeis's judgment in a few situations, there is no doubt where his sympathies lay; he, too, saw Brandeis as larger than life.

Indeed, why not, for Louis D. Brandeis is a figure to admire, and there is an air of high drama surrounding his life and career. A successful commercial lawyer turned urban reformer in an age of reform; the organizer of the first people's lobby and a successful crusader at local, state, and national levels; a legal innovator and perhaps the greatest litigation attorney of his day; a late convert to Zionism who reformulated its premises so as to make it respectable in the United States; and finally, crowning his career, a justice on the United States Supreme Court where, in his twenty-three years of service, he firmly established his reputation as one of the truly great justices in our history. Even those who have criticized other aspects of his work and thought acknowledge his greatness as a judge;[13] his opinions and dissents continue to be cited by contemporary courts as authoritative, an honor that few of his contemporaries—even the Olympian Holmes—now enjoy. For it was Brandeis who pointed the way in the most important jurisprudential development of this century, the application of the Bill of Rights to the states by incorporating its provisions through the Fourteenth Amendment.[14]

By the late sixties, however, the liberalism that had dominated American political life since the New Deal had begun to crumble, in part because of its own excesses and in part because of the Vietnam War. The optimism that lay at the core of liberalism, the belief that positive government could remedy societal evils, that social engineering could improve men and women, and that persistent maladies such as racism and poverty could be eradicated—all came to be viewed not only as passé but as wrongheaded. Instead of Franklin Roosevelt, Harry Truman, or John Kennedy with their calls to make a better America, we got Richard Nixon, Jimmy Carter, and Ronald Reagan, all of whom castigated the government and called for the reduction or even the elimination of programs that reformers had spent a half-century putting into place.

With this sea-change in the political world came a scholarly reexamination of the theoretical ideas and constructs that had dominated public discourse for five decades. With a newly invigorated defense of the free enterprise system, attention turned to Brandeis's castigation of monopoly and his attacks on what he termed "the curse of bigness." His condemnation of industrial giants as subversive of political freedom, his charge that bigness in business inevitably led to inefficiency and corruption, and his call for a return to a small-unit, highly competitive market had been applauded by reformers since the early years of this century, and for many liberals big business constituted *the* greatest threat to American democracy. But many scholars now asked whether these views made any economic sense, not only in the seventies, but even at the time Brandeis had first put them forward.[15]

The revision began with Richard Abrams's examination of the New Haven–Boston & Maine merger fight.[16] The standard view explicated by Mason in both the biography and a separate monograph portrayed Brandeis as opposing J.P. Morgan's grab for power on behalf of a duped citizenry.[17] The citizenry had to have been duped, for otherwise, Mason could not account for the large number of responsible and supposedly hardheaded businessmen who opposed Brandeis and supported the merger. Abrams made a convincing case that New England businessmen needed a more rational and unified transportation system in order to remain competitive in a rapidly changing national market.

Similarly, James Penick[18] has suggested that the Pinchot-Ballinger controversy, in which, again according to the Mason account,[19] Brandeis exposed the anticonservation plots of the Taft administration, may not have been quite so simple. In fact, Secretary Ballinger's overall proposal for the use of public resources made a great deal of economic sense and bore a striking resemblance to the plans adopted a generation later during the New Deal.

Abrams and Penick did not, it should be noted, ascribe either evil intentions or stupidity to Brandeis; rather, they suggested that his set of economic assumptions did not necessarily correspond to the new demands of a swiftly evolving macroeconomy. Albro Martin, on the other hand, condemned Brandeis for his allegedly self-righteous criticism of corporate managers whose good intentions and historical rightness Martin took as self-evident.[20] In less vitriolic terms, Gabriel Kolko believed Brandeis's emphasis on efficiency led him to miss the real issue, the realignment of power.[21]

A rather strange and even more ill-tempered version of the Martin view appeared in an article in *Harper's Magazine* by L.J. Davis, entitled "Other People's Money: How Justice Brandeis Almost Ruined the Country." It is a tendentious and error-studded piece, which claims that after Morgan had "single-handedly stopped the great panic of 1907, it became clear to certain thoughtful men that the order he had produced was good, and that to return to the dubious blessings of capitalism unchained was unthinkable." Unfortunately, Louis Brandeis was not one of these "thoughtful" men, and he proceeded to attack the great financier, according to Davis, as though 120 years of economic development had never occurred.[22]

The most sustained and well-reasoned attack on Brandeisian economics has come from Thomas McCraw, in an article in *The American Scholar* and in his Pulitzer Prize–winning *Prophets of Regulation*.[23] McCraw correctly identifies the roots of Brandeis's economic thought in a Jeffersonian view of society and also, I believe correctly, notes that action rather than philosophic consideration marked Brandeis's career before 1916. McCraw argues: "Brandeis's emphasis on the 'curse of bigness' proved to be an illogical principle on which to base realistic remedies for the ills of modern life. . . . Certainly it is of little help in shaping economic policy. In the case of business organizations, bigness is indeed a curse for some industries (leather, apparel, food service); but for others (steel, oil, automobiles), it represents not only a virtue but an inevitability."[24] Research in all disciplines, according to McCraw, as well as historical experience in all democratic market countries, proves this; there is a cluster of industries across a scale, and all efforts to move industries away from their natural cluster, to make small business large or large business small, have had little success.

I am prepared to concede a number of economic points to McCraw and the others who argue about the inevitability of bigness in certain sectors of the economy, as well as to agree that size in and of itself is not the sole criterion we should use in judging either the economic or the social utility of industry. This, I should add, is hardly a radical or a treacherous statement; Walter Lippmann, Harold Laski, and Adolf Berle, all of whom admired Brandeis greatly, condemned his economic thought as wrongheaded or, in Laski's elegant words, as "a nobly romantic anachronism."[25]

But Brandeis himself never claimed to be an economist and, aside from his perhaps overexaggerated faith in the panacea of efficiency, never proposed any economic guidelines for business control or development. Rather, we should view

Brandeis's strictures against bigness in moral terms; further, we must view them not in the light of contemporary economic thought but in the context in which Brandeis himself worked and wrote, America in the age of industrialization.[26]

The debate over the rightness or wrongness of Brandeis's economic views is largely irrelevant in assessing the man, as is the related debate over the wisdom or futility of American antitrust policy. Brandeis responded, as did so many of the Progressives, to the moral, social, and political strains that the new industrial giants placed on the system. Brandeis worried about opportunity, about preserving a type of society in which ambitious and talented persons could, through hard work and ability, be able to make their fame and fortune. He despaired about the ability of democracy to survive in a system where everybody worked for large, impersonal corporations with little hope of personal success or independence.

I, for one, do not believe these concerns to be irrelevant. The terms of the debate have changed, and Brandeis certainly did underestimate the ability of the economy to generate new opportunities for individual enterprise. In the light of recent headlines about corporate greed and the social irresponsibility of large, multinational corporations, however, it would seem that the questions Brandeis raised three-quarters of a century ago should still be of concern. We need not accept his solutions to recognize the validity of the questions; in fact, Brandeis made it quite clear on a number of occasions that people had to devise their own solutions to social problems. That was what democracy was—and is—all about.

A second area in which Brandeis has figured as a center of controversy involves his extrajudicial activities and the alleged "scandals" uncovered by Bruce Allen Murphy in *The Brandeis/Frankfurter Connection.*[27] My differences with Professor Murphy are well known and need not be reiterated here.[28] The book, however, as well as Nelson Dawson's more limited study of their collaboration,[29] does raise legitimate questions about the nature of the judicial role, the controlling ethics of those who sit on our nation's highest court, and the role that judges should or should not play in the larger political arena. It also raises questions about the ethical obligations of law professors, and to some people Felix Frankfurter's role as Brandeis's surrogate involved more complex and more disturbing issues. Judges, after all, have been extrajudicially involved in the political process since the founding of the nation.

Here again, I do not wish to defend Bandeis by claiming that because of his personal integrity we can be sure that he did not abuse either powers of his office or the trust reposed in him. Nor is it enough to note that the standards of judicial conduct have changed in the last fifty years and that if Brandeis were alive today he would no doubt adhere to the current strictures on judicial activity. In an essay I wrote many years ago, I pointed out that if, in the matter of his political involvement while a judge, we hold him up to his own professed standards he falls short.[30] It is regrettable, but also somewhat reassuring, to find human traits such as fallibility in his character.

The debate over Brandeis's economic beliefs and the integrity of his extrajudicial conduct will, I am sure, continue to be debated so long as we continue to recognize Louis Brandeis as one of the important figures in the legal and political history of modern America. But I believe there are more fruitful avenues of research for scholars to pursue. Let me suggest four areas where I think we need new, fresh approaches.

Reform: The criticism of Brandeis's economic views should lead us to reexamine reform activity before World War I in general, as well as his role in particular. Unlike the "good guys/bad guys" view that permeated so much of the early writing on progressivism, we are now beginning to understand the complexities and variety of reform. Rather than talk about a single progressivism, we acknowledge the existence of many progressive strands, together making up an enormously rich tapestry.[31]

How we view that tapestry, what threads and patterns we wish to focus upon, depends on our predilections and interests. Some of us may approach it through an interest in women's history, and Brandeis appears to have been one of the few male reformers with extensive ties into the circle of women reformers such as Florence Kelly.[32] Or we may choose to explore labor history or the reformation of governmental process or the structural nature of business.

It has long been my view that progressivism can best be understood through the individuals who led discrete reforms and through those who served as "linchpins" of reform, tying together those with relatively narrow interests into more powerful coalitions.[33] If there is anything that the *Letters* show clearly, it is Brandeis's extensive contacts with dozens of reform movements and literally hundreds of people. Part of his strength as a reformer can be traced to this network of contacts that he created.

What we need are monographic studies of some of Brandeis's particular reform efforts, but viewed in broad context. Mason's study of savings bank life insurance,[34] for example, is too narrowly focused, concentrating almost entirely on Brandeis and ignoring a number of factors, such as the labor union agenda, the economic and political reasons so many savings banks proved reluctant to join the system, and the role of other activists. Brandeis's role is heroic enough, but he could not have done it alone; he needed and sought allies, and the institutional structure he created served him well as a model in later reform.

The suggestions of McCraw and others that Brandeis's economic ideas lacked validity need to be examined not only in the light of what we know today about economic theory and development but also in the context of the times. More important, we need to understand what Brandeis strove for in terms of ultimate goals. It may be too facile to summarize his views by saying he wanted to reestablish a small-unit, competitive economy to undergird a small-unit, Jeffersonian society.

Everything we have learned about Brandeis indicates his hardheadedness, especially about facing up to facts. He was not emotionless; to the contrary, he cared much and cared deeply. But as he once told his daughter Susan, she would do well to remember that "life is hard."[35] These are not the words of a Luddite, a man who would ignore the economic and social facts of life to chase a chimera. He also chose his words carefully, so we cannot and ought not to assume that he meant something other than what he actually said. The task is to ascertain not only what he said, which, given the large record he left for us, is fairly simple, but also what he intended. I have a suspicion that as we do this there may be more to the Brandeisian vision than we have realized so far. The suggestions made by Philippa Strum, for example, on the impact that Alfred Zimmern's *The Greek Commonwealth* had on Brandeis[36] might fruitfully be followed through with an emphasis on the meaning of balance in one's personal life as well as in that of the state.

Zionism: A second area that requires additional research is Brandeis's involvement in the Zionist movement. It is difficult to recall that in 1965 not a single historical work had been written about American Zionism. Although the movement occupied much of Brandeis's time and thought for the last thirty years of his life, Mason devoted only two thin chapters to Brandeis's involvement, and it is clear that Mason understood neither the movement nor the reasons for Brandeis's interest.

There are two aspects of Brandeis's Zionism that have received scholarly attention, what we might call the *how* and the *why*. I have argued that in terms of *how*, we can view the Brandeisian era in American Zionism as an extension of his reform work.[37] "Men! Money! Discipline!" became the motto of Zionism in this country, just as it had been for savings bank insurance, monetary overhaul, and a dozen other activities. More important, the Brandeisian synthesis, which rephrased the goal of a modern Jewish homeland in Palestine in terms of American ideas, made Zionism respectable in the United States, not only to assimilated Jews, but to non-Jews as well. Insofar as the *how* is concerned, I think the thesis has held up pretty well. Some scholars have criticized certain points and clarified others, but the essential argument of Brandeisian Zionism as a variety of American progressive reform remains valid.

The second part of the question, *why* Brandeis became a Zionist, remains unanswered. In 1971 Yonathan Shapiro suggested an application of Everett Stonequist's theory of marginal man to the Brandeis group.[38] By this thesis, members of groups that are marginal to mainstream society and who are rejected in their efforts to achieve respectability in the host society will turn inward and take leadership roles among their own people. Brandeis, according to Shapiro, failed to win the status his talents should have brought him, first in Boston and then in the country at large, because he was Jewish; as a result of anti-Semitism, therefore, he returned to his people and became their leader.

Shapiro, however, had very little evidence to support his claim that Brandeis had suffered from anti-Semitism; in 1980 Allon Gal's *Brandeis of Boston* offered some proof that Brandeis had, indeed, been discriminated against because of his nominal religion.[39]

I remain unconvinced. Even conceding Brandeis's reticence over personal matters, there is very little in his papers, including the recently opened cache of over two thousand personal items to his family, that could be interpreted to show that Brandeis felt the type of suffering Shapiro claims is necessary to cause the marginal person to turn inward. That prejudice existed is undeniable, but that it was *the* causal factor in leading Brandeis to Zionism is difficult for me to accept. Even in the fight over Brandeis's confirmation to the Supreme Court, anti-Semitism played a very minor role in the opposition, and by then Brandeis had become the established leader of the movement in America.[40]

Ben Halpern and a few others have suggested that Brandeis had never really strayed far from a commitment to Judaism, and they point to the Frankist background of his family.[41] Even if the ritual of Judaism had been ignored in his Louisville home (as it would be in his Boston home as well), Fredericka and Adolph instilled in him the prophetic teachings of justice and mercy.

Such a thesis is incapable of proof one way or the other. The prophetic ideals of Judaism, as Brandeis often pointed out, differed little from those of Thomas Jefferson's deistic humanism. In her memoirs, Fredericka wrote that she had never believed in any formal religion and had raised her children to appreciate the beauty of all religions without being committed to any particular form.[42] Brandeis never denied his Jewish birth, but at least before 1910 he seems to have considered it akin to brown eyes or black hair, an accident of birth, with no special significance.

The works of Shapiro, Gal, and Halpern must certainly be taken into account if we are ever to discover *why* Brandeis became a Zionist. Unless there still remains one more hidden cache of letters, we will not find any new or startling revelations, and we will have to fall back on his own explanation— that in Zionism, Brandeis found the noblest ideals of the American heritage—without dismissing this as apologetic rhetoric.

There is, however, still much research that can be done, on both the *how* and the *why*. Some of Brandeis's chief lieutenants, such as Julian Mack, the Flexners, Abba Hillel Silver, and Felix Frankfurter, either lack good biographies or have had their Zionist work relegated to a secondary role.[43] We need to know more about the interaction of the various Zionist groups and how the imperative for Americanization affected their Zionist ideas. Brandeis, whom his law partner once described as more Brahmin than the Brahmins,[44] must have presented an awesome figure to the Yiddish-speaking Socialists of the East Side. And, of course, we do need to know more about anti-Semitism and how—if at all—it affected Brandeis and his associates.

The Law: Not surprisingly, much of the early scholarly literature on Brandeis dealt with his commitment to "a living law." His 1905 speech to the Harvard Ethical Society, a talk that greatly influenced the young Felix Frankfurter, is still considered a classic.[45] Allon Gal has drawn a good portrait of the clientele Brandeis served in his law practice,[46] and that information has given us considerable insight into other facets of Brandeis's career and thought. There has been little analysis of his work as a litigator, but it is clear from contemporary accounts—especially from those whom he bested in legal combat—that Brandeis may have been the greatest courtroom lawyer of his time.

From the time he took his seat on the high court in 1916, law review writers paid close attention to his opinions and especially to his dissents. During the reaction of the twenties, liberals looked to him and to Holmes to sustain the liberal viewpoint; in the thirties they relied, not always to their satisfaction, on Brandeis, Benjamin Cardozo, and Harlan Fiske Stone to justify the economic experimentation of the New Deal. By the time he retired from the Court in 1939, even those who had been among his bitterest critics at the time of his nomination applauded him as one of the great jurists in the history of the Court.

In the forties and fifties, Brandeis's reputation remained high. The policy of judicial restraint that he and Holmes had defended now won adherences from the Roosevelt and Truman appointees, and the Court in practice abandoned review of economic legislation.[47] Brandeis's championing of the administrative agencies[48] and his call for courts to stop second-guessing administrative findings also became widely accepted, and the courts got out of the business of reviewing rate schedules and other commonplace bureaucratic business. His innovative use of facts in the *Muller*[49] brief became the norm in litigating social issues, and the decision in *Brown* v. *Board of Education* (1954) marks the ultimate triumph of the Brandeis brief.[50] Most important, the proposal that the Due Process Clause of the Fourteenth Amendment included the protection of civil liberties developed into the doctrine of incorporation, and courts began playing an activist role in protecting civil rights and civil liberties, a role Brandeis had urged upon them in the twenties.

Ironically, one area where Brandeis's jurisprudence received less than enthusiastic applause involved a seeming triumph, his overturn of federal common law in *Erie Railroad* v. *Tompkins* (1938).[51] Within a few years, however, courts began "interpreting" Brandeis's call for federal court deference to state decisional rules in such a way as to effectively negate *Erie*.[52]

In the late sixties and early seventies, as liberalism collapsed, the reputation of "liberal" judges such as Brandeis inevitably came in for reappraisal. G. Edward White, in his thoughtful study of the American judicial tradition, noted that "Brandeis was a liberal in his result orientation only to the extent that liberalism endorsed Brandeisian social policies; he was a liberal in methodology only to the extent that judicial self-restraint fostered results he thought sensible."[53] In short, Brandeis allowed his own prejudices to affect his judging. When first Dawson and then Murphy "exposed" Brandeis's extrajudicial involvements, it appeared to many that under the black robes their hero had feet of clay.

By this time a number of writers had begun to reexamine Brandeis's life and work and especially his contributions on the bench. Thomas McCraw, who has been so critical of Brandeis as an economic reformer, nonetheless considers him "a truly great judge," whose tenure was marked by "impartiality, wisdom and judicial depth."[54] David Levy argued convincingly for an inescapable integrity that ran through Brandeis's entire career.[55] Alexander Bickel's brilliant analysis of Brandeis's suppressed opinions showed how well the justice could play the political court game,[56] while Bickel's trenchant critiques of judicial activism refurbished, at least partially, the Holmes/Brandeis/Frankfurter philosophy of judicial restraint.[57]

In what is perhaps one of the most important doctrinal developments of our time, the Supreme Court has placed its imprimatur upon a constitutionally protected right of privacy, an idea first proposed by Brandeis at the end of the nineteenth century. "The right to be let alone," he later proclaimed in the thirties, is the greatest of all rights and "the one most cherished by civilized man."[58]

It should not surprise us that liberal jurists such as William O. Douglas would quote Brandeis in this area, but so have conservatives such as Warren E. Burger.[59] In the thirties Brandeis's warnings about the dangers of government surveillance, especially through the use of modern technology, were dismissed as farfetched by his contemporaries;[60] in the eighties we know that he barely hinted at the possibilities of electronic intrusion into home and office.

For all that has been written on Brandeis the Judge, however, it may be that the best is yet to come. Brandeis gave his reform and Zionist papers to the University of Louisville Law Library, but he entrusted his court records to Felix Frankfurter, who guarded them jealously and refused to allow Alpheus Mason access. Frankfurter deposited the papers in the Harvard Law School but kept them sealed. He later turned control over to Paul Freund, one of his former pupils and a Brandeis clerk, indicating that he expected Freund to write *the* biography of their common mentor. Frankfurter also allowed his own clerk, Bickel, in to study the unpublished opinions.

These papers are finally available to all scholars, not only at Harvard, but in a microfilm edition as well.[61] Bickel used some of them in the last work he did, the volume on the Edward Douglass White Court for the Holmes Device;[62] no doubt the authors who will write on the Taft and Hughes courts will find much of value there as well. With this, the last major known collection of Brandeis papers now open, we should be able to learn a great deal about the Court and about one of its greatest members.

Personal Life: A final area where much work remains is Brandeis the Man. Because he valued privacy so highly, none of the early works included very much information on his personal affairs. The family doled out a relatively small amount of private papers to Mason, and his daughters gave only a marginal number of notes to the *Letters* project. These few, and for the most part impersonal, items distorted our view of Brandeis. Some people, noting that Brandeis's letters to his wife read like law briefs, and Brandeis briefs at that, concluded that the austere public personality reflected an equally cold private nature, a conclusion that the available evidence seemed to confirm.

Certainly, the Brandeis family lived simply and far below the material style that his ample income could have provided. Brandeis just had little use for the frivolous or the merely decorative; in food, clothing, and shelter, he preferred the simple and utilitarian. He did not like telephones or automobiles and did not even want to own property; he only bought his summer home on Cape Cod because the owner, from whom he had previously rented, threatened to sell it to someone else. Dinner at the Brandeises was simple to the point of being spartan. Julian Mack, a lover of fine food, once commented that when you went to the Brandeises' for dinner you had to eat beforehand and then again afterward.

Following the death of Susan Brandeis Gilbert, her family discovered a cache of about 2,500 letters written by Brandeis to his wife and daughters over a fifty-year period. So far, only one person, Lewis J. Paper, has exploited this collection,[63] but it will be essential to future scholars. We now have the material to examine a number of aspects of Brandeis's family life and can try to extrapolate how certain events, such as the frequent hospitalization of his wife for depression, affected his life and career. We know very little about either Susan or Elizabeth before they entered on their own public careers; the Gilbert Papers give us an entirely new and quite surprising portrait of them as girls and young women. Susan, it turns out, had a wild romantic streak that caused her parents much anxiety.

The Enduring Brandeis

Having much, of course, makes one want more, and this appears true for Brandeis scholarship as well. Within the past few years, we have seen several new biographies, each of which makes a significant contribution to our understanding of the man. In the next few years, we can expect to see two more volumes of letters, one incorporating the Frankfurter material and the other consisting of family papers, primarily from the Gilbert collection. The ongoing debate over Brandeis's economic views has generated a number of pieces and shows little sign of abating. The opening of his court papers will facilitate the work of several people who are now engaged in writing about his judicial career.

But all of these works are like pieces in a puzzle, and the sum in this case is surely greater than the parts. At some point we will have all of the pieces in place, and then Louis Brandeis will finally get the biography that he—and we— deserve.

I have no doubt that the pieces and the biography will be written, for the enduring interest in Brandeis rests on far more than his success as a reformer or his brilliance as a judge, and his reputation will easily withstand the carpings of economic critics or those who think he sullied the judicial ermine.

Brandeis's appeal rests not only on what he accomplished but on what he tried to do, namely bridging the values of a passing era to the still vague assumptions of a new time. He did not know all the dangers or rewards that the new era would offer, and his critics miss the mark when they complain that he misunderstood industrialized modern society. He never claimed to have all the right questions. Some of these may not be as burning as they were in his day, but the underlying themes are still there.

If we have won the battle to eliminate child labor and to establish fair wages and hours, we have still not resolved the appropriate relationship between giant corporations and their individual workers.

If the worst abuses of monopoly have been abated by antitrust laws, the issue of large-scale concentration of economic power is still with us, in the form of multinational corporations and conglomerates.

If the Supreme Court has recognized the existence of a constitutionally protected right to privacy, the limits and nature of that right are still far from clear.

Brandeis's emphasis on the link between morality and economics, which has been derided as irrelevant and wrongheaded, appears once again to be timely, as are his warnings of the dire consequences that result when government officials break the law in the name of some "higher good."

With such great concern over the role of activist courts, we may do well to look anew at his views on judicial restraint and the limits of judicial power.

And with the relationship between American Jewry and Israel so strained, the ideas of a collaborative kinship that he articulated might well provide the basis for rethinking the nature of Zionism as well as ties between Israel and the Diaspora.

Perhaps this is why I keep coming back to the man, to his

life and work. On several occasions I thought I had finished, and each time I would run across something new, a letter or an opinion or a source I had not seen before, and suddenly there would be a new idea, a new appreciation of what he stood for. I am not done exploring Brandeis, but it is a vast territory, and those of us working there welcome company.

1. Arthur S. Link, *Wilson: The Road to the White House* (Princeton: Princeton Univ. Press, 1947), 489.

2. The material on the Brandeis-Wilson relationship is presented in Melvin I. Urofsky, "Wilson, Brandeis, and the Trust Issue, 1912-1914," *Mid-America* 49 (1967): 3.

3. Melvin I. Urofsky and David W. Levy, eds., *The Letters of Louis D. Brandeis*, 5 vols. (Albany: State Univ. of New York Press, 1971-78) (abbreviated hereafter as BL). Two additional volumes are now in preparation, one containing the letters to Felix Frankfurter and the other the newfound family papers.

4. Melvin I. Urofsky, *Louis D. Brandeis and the Progressive Tradition* (Boston: Little, Brown, 1980).

5. Melvin I. Urofsky, *American Zionism from Herzl to the Holocaust* (Garden City, N.Y.: Anchor Press/Doubleday, 1975); *We Are One! American Jewry and Israel* (Garden City, N.Y.: Anchor Press/Doubleday, 1978).

6. *A Voice That Spoke for Justice: The Life and Times of Stephen S. Wise* (Albany: State Univ. of New York Press, 1981); a study of Frankfurter is now under way for the Twayne series of twentieth-century biography.

7. See, for example, "Zionism: Toward the Year 2000," *Midstream* 24 (Feb. 1978): 66; and "The Twenty-ninth Zionist Congress," ibid. 36 (April 1978) and 63 (May 1978).

8. BL, I:xx.

9. A relatively comprehensive list of books and articles about Brandeis up until 1958 is found in Roy M. Mersky, *Louis Dembitz Brandeis, 1856-1941: A Bibliography* (New Haven: Yale Law School, 1958). The list had not changed significantly when we began our work in 1965.

10. Jacob de Haas, *Louis D. Brandeis: A Biographical Sketch* (New York: Bloch Publishing Co., 1929).

11. Alfred Lief, *Brandeis: The Personal History of an American Ideal* (New York: Stackpole, 1936).

12. Alpheus T. Mason, *Brandeis: Lawyer and Judge in the Modern State* (Princeton: Princeton Univ. Press, 1933); and idem, *The Brandeis Way* (Princeton: Princeton Univ. Press, 1938).

13. After criticizing Brandeis's economic views, for example, Thomas K. McCraw writes that "once on the bench, Brandeis surprised his critics with his wisdom and judicial depth. He made a great judge, one of the most distinguished in American history" ("Louis D. Brandeis Reappraised," *American Scholar* 54 [1985]:525, 531).

14. *Gilbert v. Minnesota*, 254 U.S. 325, 343 (1920) (dissenting).

15. A comprehensive overview of this literature is L.S. Zacharias, "Repaving the Brandeis Way," manuscript courtesy of Professor Zacharias.

16. Richard M. Abrams, "Brandeis and the New Haven–Boston & Maine Merger Battle Revisited," *Business History Review* 36 (1962):408; expanded and somewhat revised in Abrams, *Conservatism in a Progressive Era: Massachusetts Politics, 1900-1912* (Cambridge, Mass.: Harvard Univ. Press, 1964).

17. Henry Staples and Alpheus T. Mason, *The Fall of a Railroad Empire: Brandeis and the New Haven Merger Battle* (Syracuse: Syracuse Univ. Press, 1947).

18. James L. Penick, Jr., *Progressive Politics and Conservation: The Ballinger-Pinchot Affair* (Chicago: Univ. of Chicago Press, 1968).

19. *Bureaucracy Convicts Itself* (New York: Viking Press, 1941).

20. Albro Martin, *Enterprise Denied: Origins of the Decline of the American Railroads, 1897-1917* (New York: Columbia Univ. Press, 1971).

21. Gabriel Kolko, *The Triumph of Conservatism: A Reinterpretation of American History, 1900-1916* (New York: Free Press, 1963).

22. *Harper's*, 268 Feb. 1984:62.

23. McCraw, "Louis D. Brandeis"; idem, *Prophets of Regulation: Charles Francis Adams, Louis D. Brandeis, James M. Landis, and Alfred E. Kahn* (Cambridge, Mass.: Harvard Univ. Press, 1984).

24. McCraw, "Louis D. Brandeis," 527.

25. Walter Lippmann, *Drift and Mastery* (New York: M. Kennerly, 1914); Adolph A. Berle, Jr., and Gardiner Means, *The Modern Corporation and Private Property* (New York: Macmillan, 1932); Harold Laski, "Mr. Justice Brandeis," *Harper's*, 168 Jan. 1934:209.

26. Melvin I. Urofsky, *A Mind of One Piece: Brandeis and American Reform* (New York: Charles Scribner's Sons, 1971), chap.2.

27. Bruce Allen Murphy, *The Brandeis/Frankfurter Connection: The Secret Political Activities of Two Supreme Court Justices* (New York: Oxford Univ. Press, 1982).

28. "Mountains and Molehills," *Moment* 8 (June 1983):52.

29. Nelson L. Dawson, *Louis D. Brandeis, Felix Frankfurter, and the New Deal* (Hamden, Conn.: Archon Books, 1980).

30. Urofsky, *Mind of One Piece*, 129-30.

31. See, for example, Robert Wiebe, *The Search for Order, 1877-1920* (New York: Hill and Wang, 1967).

32. Josephine C. Goldmark, *Impatient Crusader: Florence Kelly's Life Story* (Urbana: Univ. of Illinois Press, 1953).

33. Urofsky, *Mind of One Piece*, chap. 7.

34. Mason, *Brandeis Way*.

35. Urofsky, *Brandeis and the Progressive Tradition*, 168.

36. Philippa Strum, *Louis D. Brandeis: Justice for the People* (Cambridge, Mass.: Harvard Univ. Press, 1984), 237-42.

37. "Zionism: An American Experience," *American Jewish Historical Quarterly* 63 (1974):215; expanded in Urofsky, *American Zionism*.

38. Yonathan Shapiro, *Leadership of the American Zionist Organization, 1897-1930* (Urbana: Univ. of Illinois Press, 1972).

39. Allon Gal, *Brandeis of Boston* (Cambridge, Mass.: Harvard Univ. Press, 1979).

40. There are two thick files of letters to Woodrow Wilson (Wilson Papers, Manuscript Division of the Library of Congress) commenting upon the Brandeis nomination. Only a handful of the writers opposed Brandeis because of his religion; most of the opposition focused on his allegedly "radical" economic views.

41. Ben Halpern, "Brandeis's Way to Zionism," *Midstream* 17 (Oct. 1971):3.

42. Frederika Brandeis, *Reminiscences*, trans. Alice G. Brandeis (privately printed, 1943), 33.

43. Michael Parrish, *Felix Frankfurter and His Times: The Reform Years* (New York: Free Press, 1982), does have one chapter on his Zionist activities; Harry Barnard, *The Life and Times of Judge Julian Mack* (New York: Herzl Press, 1974), is an encomium to the man, but lacks historical analysis. There is nothing substantial on the Flexners, and while one hears periodic rumors that someone or the other is at work on a biography of Silver, so far nothing has appeared.

44. Urofsky, *Mind of One Piece*, 3.

45. "The Opportunity in the Law," *American Law Review* 39 (1905):555.

46. Gal, *Brandeis of Boston*, chap. 1.

47. *Williamson* v. *Lee Optical Company*, 348 U.S. 483 (1955).

48. *Pacific Statutes Box & Basket Co.* v. *White*, 296 U.S. 176 (1935).

49. *Muller* v. *Oregon*, 208 U.S. 412 (1908).

50. 347 U.S. 483 (1954).

51. 304 U.S. 64 (1938).

52. See the discussion of problems generated by *Erie* in David P. Currie, *Federal Courts: Cases and Materials* (St. Paul, Minn.: West Publishing Co., 1982), 392-97.

53. G. Edward White, *The American Judicial Tradition* (New York: Oxford Univ. Press, 1976), 176.

54. McCraw, "Louis D. Brandeis."

55. "The Lawyer as Judge: Brandeis' View of the Legal Profession," *Oklahoma Law Review* 22 (1969):374.

56. *The Unpublished Opinions of Mr. Justice Brandeis* (Cambridge, Mass.: Harvard Univ. Press, 1957).

57. Alexander M. Bickel, *The Least Dangerous Branch: The Supreme Court at the Bar of Politics*, rev. ed. (New Haven: Yale Univ. Press, 1981).

58. *Olmstead* v. *United States*, 277 U.S. 438, 478 (1928) (dissenting).

59. *In re President of Georgetown College*, 331 F.2d 1000, 1015 (D.C. Cir. 1964) (dissenting).

60. *Olmstead.*

61. American Legal Manuscripts, *The Louis Dembitz Brandeis Papers* (Frederick, Md.: University Microfilms, 1985).

62. Alexander M. Bickel and Benno C. Schmidt, Jr., *The Judiciary and Responsible Government, 1910-1921* (New York: Macmillan, 1984).

63. Lewis J. Paper, *Brandeis* (Englewood Cliffs, NJ.: Prentice-Hall, 1983).

Suggested Reading

JANET B. HODGSON

Alexander, Constantine, et al. *Nutter, McClennen & Fish: The First Century, 1879-1979*. Privately Printed, 1979.

Baker, Leonard. *Brandeis and Frankfurter: A Dual Biography*. New York: Harper & Row, 1984.

Bickel, Alexander M., ed. *The Unpublished Opinions of Mr. Justice Brandeis*. Cambridge, Mass.: Harvard Univ. Press, 1957.

Burt, Robert A. *Two Jewish Justices: Outcasts in the Promised Land*. Berkeley: Univ. of California Press, 1988.

Danelski, David J. *A Supreme Court Justice Is Appointed*. New York: Random House, 1964.

Dawson, Nelson L. *Louis D. Brandeis, Felix Frankfurter, and the New Deal*. Hamden, Conn.: Archon Books, 1980.

Gal, Allon. *Brandeis of Boston*. Cambridge, Mass.: Harvard Univ. Press, 1980.

Halpern, Ben. *A Clash of Heroes: Brandeis, Weizmann, and American Zionism*. New York: Oxford Univ. Press, 1987.

McCraw, Thomas K. *Prophets of Regulation*. Cambridge, Mass.: Belknap Press of Harvard Univ. Press, 1984.

Mason, Alpheus T. *Brandeis: A Free Man's Life*. New York: Viking Press, 1946, 1956 [Anniversary Edition].

Mersky, Roy. *Louis Dembitz Brandeis, 1856-1941: A Bibliography*. New Haven, Conn.: Yale Law School, 1958: reprinted Littleton, Colo.: Fred B. Rothman, 1988.

Murphy, Bruce Allen. *The Brandeis/Frankfurter Connection*. New York: Oxford Univ. Press, 1982.

Paper, Lewis J. *Brandeis*. Englewood Cliffs, N.J.: Prentice-Hall, 1983.

Strum, Philippa. *Louis D. Brandeis: Justice for the People.* Cambridge, Mass.: Harvard Univ. Press, 1984.

Teitelbaum, Gene. *Justice Louis D. Brandeis: A Bibliography of Writings and Other Materials on the Justice.* Littleton, Colo.: Fred B. Rothman, 1988.

Todd, Alden L. *Justice on Trial: The Case of Louis D. Brandeis.* New York: McGraw-Hill, 1964.

Urofsky, Melvin I. *A Mind of One Piece: Brandeis and American Reform,* New York: Scribner's, 1971.

Urofsky, Melvin I., and Levy, David W., eds. *The Letters of Louis D. Brandeis.* 5 vols. Albany: State Univ. of New York Press, 1971– .

Contributors

DAVID J. DANELSKI, a political scientist and lawyer, is Mary Lou and George Boone Centennial Professor at Stanford University and director of Stanford in Washington. He is the author of *A Supreme Court Justice Is Appointed* (1964) and *Rights, Liberties and Ideals* (1983). He also edited (with Joseph Tulchin) *The Autobiographical Notes of Charles Evans Hughes* (1973).

NELSON L. DAWSON is publications editor for the Filson Club Historical Society. He is co-editor of *A Kentucky Sampler: Essays from the Filson Club History Quarterly, 1926-1976* (1977) and author of *Louis D. Brandeis, Felix Frankfurter, and the New Deal* (1980) as well as several articles on Brandeis and other topics in twentieth-century American history.

JANET B. HODGSON is associate archivist at the University of Louisville, where she has responsibility for technical services. A co-editor of the *Guide to the Papers of Louis Dembitz Brandeis at the University of Louisville, Microfilm Edition*, she also edited the D. W. Griffith Papers and the Henry Watterson Papers for microfilm.

ALLON GAL, born in Israel, is a professor of history at the Institute of Contemporary Jewry at the Hebrew University at Jerusalem. He is the author of *Socialist-Zionism* (1973), *Brandeis of Boston* (1980), and *David Ben-Gurion and the American Alignment for a Jewish State* (1984) as well as numerous articles in twentieth-century American Jewish history, Zionism, and American themes.

DAVID W. LEVY is David Ross Boyd Professor of American History at the University of Oklahoma. He is co-editor of *The Letters of Louis D. Brandeis* (1971–) and author of *Herbert Croly of the New Republic: The Life and Thought of an American Progressive* (1985).

PHILIPPA STRUM teaches political science at the City University of New York and is the author of *Presidential Power and American Democracy* (1972), *The Supreme Court and "Political Questions"* (1974), and *Louis D. Brandeis: Justice for the People* (1984) in addition to other books and numerous articles. She is active in the area of civil liberties, particularly as a member of the board of directors and executive committee of the American Civil Liberties Union.

MELVIN I. UROFSKY is currently professor of history at Virginia Commonwealth University in Richmond; he holds a Ph.D. from Columbia University and a law degree from the University of Virginia. In addition to his work as co-editor of *The Brandeis Letters*, he has written a biography of Brandeis, a history of American Zionism, and several works on legal history. His latest work is *A March of Liberty: American Constitutional and Legal History* (1988). He is now at work on a study of the Supreme Court from 1953 to 1986.

Index

Throughout the index, Louis D. Brandeis is referred to by his initials (LDB), and Franklin Delano Roosevelt is referred to as FDR.

Abrams, Richard, 136
Acheson, Dean, 119
Agricultural Adjustment Administration (AAA), LDB's opposition to, 19, 20, 41, 44, 45, 51
agriculture, LDB's interest in, 45. *See also* farmers
Ahad Ha'am, 74-75
American Bar Association, code of judicial ethics, 15
American Lumber case, 8
American Zionism. *See* Zionism, American anti-Semitism, 69, 76-77, 80, 142
Avukah (Torch) (American Zionist students' organization), 90-94

Baker, Leonard, 2, 13, 14-15, 32-33 n 40
Balfour, Arthur, 8
Ben-Gurion, David, 82
Bentov, Mordecai, 86-88
Ben-Zvi, Shmuel, 88
Berle, Adolf A., Jr., 20-21, 43, 137
Bernstein, Philip S., 89
Bickel, Alexander M., 145, 146
big business, LDB's opposition to, 2, 20, 32 n 39, 38-39, 40, 49, 109-10, 121, 135, 138
Black, Owen, 35 n 78
Black Monday decisions of U.S. Supreme Court, 50

Blaine, James G., 105
Blaisdell, Tom, 36 n 81
Boot and Shoe Club, LDB's 1903 speech to, 105
Boston Citizenship Committee, 105
Boston Elevated Railway Co., 105
Boston Typothetae, LDB's 1904 speech to, 6, 107, 115-16 n 23
Brain Trust, 43
Brandeis, Adolph (father), 142
Brandeis, Alfred (brother), 9, 24, 45, 103, 104
Brandeis, Alice Goldmark (wife): marriage of, 5; death of, 9; knowledge of LDB's financial arrangements with Frankfurter, 22, 24; will of, 24; description of LDB's meeting with Wilson, 30 n 6; LDB's letters to, 146, 147; health of, 147
Brandeis, Elizabeth. *See* Raushenbush, Elizabeth Brandeis
Brandeis, Fredericka (mother), 142
Brandeis, Louis Dembitz: scholarship on, 1, 134; birth of, 5; education of, 5; law practice of, 5-8; as U.S. Supreme Court justice, 8, 16, 41, 53, 69, 109, 135; death of, 9, 69; personal code of propriety, 16-17, 25, 27, 28, 31 n 31, 38; will of,

Brandeis, Louis (*continued*)
24; as New Deal recruiting officer, 40, 43, 45; Judaization of, 65, 66-67, 90, 142-43; dislike of Coolidge, 83; dislike of modern world and innovations, 102-4, 111, 146-47; view of human nature, 118-19; view of the law, 119-20, 143-46. *See also* big business, LDB's opposition to; economic recovery, LDB's program for; judicial impropriety, charges against LDB; Zionism, LDB as leader in
Brandeis, Susan. *See* Gilbert, Susan Brandeis
Brandeis: A Free Man's Life (Mason, 1946), 1, 11, 134
Brandeis brief, 120, 144
Brandeis/Frankfurter Connection The (Murphy), 3, 64 n 64, 138
Brown v. *Board of Education*, 144
Bryan, William Jennings, 38
Burger, Warren E., 145
Business of the United States Supreme Court (Frankfurter and Landis), 124
Butler, Pierce, 129

Cardozo, Benjamin, 144
Carter, Jimmy, 135
Chase, Salmon P., 35 nn 73, 79
Civil Service Reform Association (Boston), 105
Clayton Antitrust Act, 112
Cleveland, Grover, 105
Cohen, Benjamin V., 46, 47, 49
Commonwealth College, LDB's donations to, 45
Coolidge, Calvin, 76, 83
Corcoran, Thomas, 26, 32 n 39, 47, 51, 64 n 60
corruption, LDB's outrage over, 104-6, 122
court reform bill, LDB's concern over, 51-53

cultural pluralism, 70
Cummings, Homer, 51, 59 n 28

Davis Chester, 45
Davis, L.J., 136-37
Dawson, Nelson L., 138, 145
de Haas, Jacob, 74, 134
Democratic party, LDB's role in drafting political statement for, 12-14, 18-19
democratic socialism, 84
Denmark, compared to Palestine, 84
"Document, The," LDB's role in drafting, 12-14, 18-19
Douglas, William O., 27, 35 n 78, 145

economic recovery, LDB's program for, 2, 40, 46, 47, 50, 136-38, 139
education, importance of to free speech, 125
Ein Ha-Shofet (Heb., The Spring of the Judge) kibbutz, 88, 91, 94
Einstein, Albert, 8
Ellis, William, 105
Emergency Relief Appropriation Act of 1935, 50
employment. *See* unemployment insurance
Epstein, Abraham, 48
Erie Railroad v. *Tompkins*, 144
Evans, Mrs. Glendower, 34 n 65

Fair Labor Standards Act, 121
farmers, LDB's concern for, 40, 45
Federal Reserve System, 112
Federal Trade Commission, 112
Federation of American Zionists, 7, 71
Filene, A. Lincoln, 27
Filene, Edward A., 6, 108
Filene, Peter, 101

First Amendment rights, 124-27
Fish, Hamilton, 35 n 73
Flexner family, 143
Florida v. *Mellon*, 26
Fourteenth Amendment, 123, 124, 135, 144
Fourth Amendment, 127-28
Frank, Jerome, 19, 20, 21, 36 n 81, 45
Frankfurter, Felix: payments made by LDB to, 3, 13, 14, 15, 21-26, 42, 138-39; Zionist activities of, 23, 42, 78, 143; and LDB's formulation of unemployment insurance policy, 26, 28, 34 n 62, 48; involvement in Sacco and Vanzetti case, 34 n 65, 42; involvement in Minimum Wage case, 36 n 81; development of friendship with LDB, 41-42; development of friendship with FDR, 42-43, 49, 52, 53; offered job of solicitor-general, 44; work on draft of Securities Act of 1933, 46; in England, 47; and LDB's tax policy, 48-49; position on court reform bill, 51-52; as U.S. Supreme Court justice, 53; description of LDB as "a mind of one piece," 118; as author, 124; Urofsky's research on, 133; as guardian of LDB's court records, 146
Frankfurter, Marion Denman (wife of Felix), 23-24
free speech and press. *See* First Amendment Rights
Freund, Paul, 99, 118, 146

Gal, Allon, 105, 142, 143
George, Henry, 100
Gilbert, Jacob (son-in-law), 9
Gilbert, Louis Brandeis (grandson), 9, 103
Gilbert, Susan Brandeis (daughter), 5, 8, 9, 24, 140, 147

Ginzberg, Asher (pseud. Ahad Ha'am), 74-75
Goldmark, Alice. *See* Brandeis, Alice Goldmark
Goldmark, Josephine (sister-in-law), 24, 120
Goldmark, Pauline (sister-in-law), 24
Goldmark, Susan, (sister-in-law), 30 n 6
Gompers, Samuel, 108
Good Government Association, 6, 105
Gottheil, Richard, 71
government: LDB's distrust of strong and big, 38-39, 41, 55, 110-11, 121, 135; Brain Trusters' view of, 43; corruption in, 105, 122
Great Britain: Mandate in Palestine, 72-73; White Paper (1939), 82, 88
Gross, David C., 13, 15

Hagannah (precursor of Israeli Defense Forces), 81
Halpern, Ben, 142, 143
halutzim (Heb., pioneers), 83
Harris, Zellig, 90, 91
Harvard Law Review, creation of, 124
Ha-Shomer Ha-Tzair kibbutz movement, 85-91, 94
Hecht, Ben, 92-93
Herzl, Theodor, 74
Hevrat Ha-Ovdim (Cooperative Society), 84
Hiss, Alger, 45
Histadruth (General Federation of Hebrew Workers in Palestine), 81, 84, 85
Hitler, Adolf, 77, 78
Holmes, Oliver Wendell, 122, 123, 124, 125, 126-27, 135, 144
Homestead strike, impact on LDB, 106
Hopkins, Harry, 62-63 n 53

Hughes, Charles Evans, 52
Humphrey's Executor v. United States, 62 n 53
Hurst, Willard, 46
Husayni, Hajj Amin al-, 78

Ickes, Harold L., 32 n 39

Jabotinsky, Vladimir Ze'ev, 73-74, 92
Jackson, Gardner, 19, 21, 36 n 81
Jay Burns Baking Company v. Bryan, 123
Jewish Agency for Palestine Executive, 82
Johnson, Alvin, 119
Johnson, Hugh, 44, 64 n 66
Judaism. See Brandeis, Louis D., Judaization of; Zionism
judicial impropriety, charges against LDB: financial arrangements with Frankfurter, 3, 13, 14, 15, 21-26, 42, 138-39; drafted "The Document," 12-14, 18-19; attempted to control legislation, 13, 15, 19-21, 26, 38; immersion in formulating policy, 14, 15, 26-29, 40-41; standards for judging, 15-18; because of political activities, 54-55

Kallen, Horace, 70, 71
Kelly, Florence, 140
Kennedy, John F., 135
Keynes, John M., 40
Kolko, Gabriel, 136

labor problems, LDB's interest in, 106-9. See also unemployment insurance
LaFollette, Robert, Sr., 7
Landis, James, 32 n 39, 46, 47, 124

Langdell, Christopher, 119
Laski, Harold, 118, 137
legislation, charge that LDB attempted to control, 13, 15, 19-21, 26, 38
Leibner, Joshua, 88, 89
Lever Act cases, 36 n 81
Levine, Daniel, 112
Levy, David W., 2, 23, 133, 134, 145
Lief, Alfred, 134
Lilienthal, David, 46
Lindheim, Irma, 85-86, 89
Lindley, Ernest, 32 n 39
Link, Arthur S., 133
Lippmann, Walter, 137
Lipsky Zionists, 106
Long, Huey, 49
Louisville Bank v. Radford, 62 n 53

McAdoo, William G., 11-12
McCraw, Thomas K., 2, 39, 137, 140, 145
McElwain, William H., 108
Mack, Julian W., 9, 23, 24, 25, 88, 104, 143, 147
McKenna, Joseph, 129
McReynolds, James, 51
Magnes, Judah, 71
Martin, Alboro, 136
Mason, Alpheus T., 1, 11-13, 18, 29, 134, 136, 141, 146
Massachusetts Election Laws League, 105
Massachusetts Society for Promoting Good Citizenship, 105
Melman, Seymour, 90
Mencken, H.L., 103
Mendes, Henry P., 71
Mind of One Piece, A (Urofsky), 2, 118
Minimum Wage case, 36 n 81
Moley, Raymond, 43, 44, 46
Morgan, J.P., 136
Morgenthau, Henry, 48

Muller v. *Oregon*, 6, 130 n 6, 144
Murphy, Bruce Allen: charges of impropriety made against LDB by, 3, 13, 19, 20, 21-23, 24, 25, 64 n 64, 138, 145

National Civic Federation, 108
National Industrial Recovery Act, 122
National Labor Relations Act, 50
National Power Policy Committee, 49
National Recovery Administration (NRA), LDB's opposition to, 20, 41, 44-45, 50-51
New Deal, first (1933): LDB's opposition to, 44-45, 46-47; LDB's satisfaction with, 46
New Deal, second (1935): Brandeisian reform as focus of, 44, 47-48, 50; LDB's disappointment with, 48; LDB's satisfaction with, 50
New Deal legislation, LDB's attempt to control, 19-21, 26, 38
New England Policy-Holders' Committee, 6
New York Garment Workers' strike (1910), 6, 7, 67, 108, 112
New York Times: coverage at Brandeis-Frankfurter arrangement by, 13, 21, 25, 26; characterization of LDB, 28; censure of LDB for attending Zionist meeting in 1916, 29
New Zionist Organization, 73, 92
Nixon, Richard M., 135
Norris, George, 46

Ohio Plan, for unemployment insurance, 48
Olmstead v. *United States*, 127-28
Other People's Money and How

the Bankers Use It (Brandeis), 8, 87, 109

Palestine, British Mandate in, 72-73, 79, 80. *See also* Zionism
Palestine Economic Corporation, 81
Palestine Economic Council, 81
Paper, Lewis J., 2, 13-14, 17, 28, 147
Passfield White Paper, 79
Penick, James, 136
Pennsylvania Coal v. *Mahon*, 123
Perkins, Frances, 27
"personalia" techniques, 42
Pierce v. *United States*, 124
Pinchot-Ballinger controversy, 6, 106, 136
Pitney, Mahlon, 129
policy, LDB's immersion in formulating, 14, 15, 26-29, 40-41
Pound, Roscoe, 122
Pressman, Lee, 36 n 81, 45
privacy, right to, 127-28, 145
Progressivism: and LDB's interest in Zionism, 3, 65, 66, 68, 76, 87, 90, 94; and LDB's interest in political and economic reform, 39, 102, 104, 107, 109, 111-13; roots of, 100-102
Provisional Executive Committee on General Zionist Affairs, LDB as chairman of, 7, 70
Public Franchise League, 6, 105
Public Utility Holding Company Act, 49
public works programs, LDB's support for, 40, 41, 49-50
Puritanism, of LDB's Zionism, 71-73

Quaker City Cab case, 9

railroad mergers, LDB's opposition to, 67, 109, 136

Ramat Ha-Shofet (Heb., The
Height of the Judge) kibbutz,
88, 94
Raushenbush, Elizabeth Brandeis (daughter), 5, 9, 24, 26,
27, 48
Raushenbush, Paul (son-in-
law), 9, 26, 48
Reagan, Ronald, 135
Report of the Commission on
the Palestine Disturbances of
August 1929 (1930), 79
Revisionism, Zionist, 73, 89, 92,
93
Riesman, David, 122
Roberts, Owen, 35 n 78
Roosevelt, Franklin Delano:
meeting with LDB, 9; and
LDB's attempt to control legislation, 19; advised by LDB,
26, 27, 38, 43-44, 46-47, 49, 53;
development of friendship
with Frankfurter, 42-43, 49,
52, 53; interest in TVA, 46; indecisiveness of, 46-47; compared to recent presidents,
135
Roosevelt, Theodore, 42, 110
Roper, Daniel, 46

Sacco and Vanzetti case, 9, 34 n
65, 36 n 81, 42, 76
savings bank life insurance,
LDB's support for, 6, 67, 108,
112, 140
Schechter v. United States, 45, 50
scientific management, 108
Securities Act of 1933, 46
Securities Exchange Act of
1934, 47
Shaefer v. United States, 125
Shapiro, Yonathan, 141-42, 143
Sharett, Moshe, 82
Sherman Antitrust Act of 1890,
49
Silver, Abba Hillel, 143
Smith, Al, 58 n 21

Social Security Act of 1935, 26,
34 n 62, 48, 121
sociological jurisprudence, 119,
124
Southern Tenant Farmers'
Union (STFU), 45
Stewart Machine Co. v. Davis,
27-28, 36 n 81
Stone, Harlan Fiske, 17, 36 n
81, 144
Stonequist, Everett, 142
Storrow, James J., 103
Strum, Philippa, 2, 13, 14, 26,
27, 141
Szold, Henrietta, 71
Szold, Robert, 77, 84

Tachau, Mary K., 118
Taft, William H., 25
Tammany Hall, 58 n 21
Taussig, James, 5
taxation, LDB's views on, 20,
40, 41, 48-49, 50
Teapot Dome scandal, 106
Tennessee Valley Authority
(TVA), 46
Thompson, Huston, 46
Truax v. Corrigan, 8, 123
Truman, Harry S., 135
Tugwell, Rexford, 2, 19, 20, 21,
43
Tumulty, Joseph P., 11-12

unemployment insurance:
LDB's role in formulating
policy for, 9, 26-27, 34 n 62,
47-48; U.S. Supreme Court
ruling on, 27-28
U.S. Constitution, LDB's interpretation of, 118, 120-24, 129.
See also First Amendment
rights; Fourteenth Amend-
ment; Fourth Amendment;
privacy, right to
U.S. Supreme Court: standards
of propriety for justices, 16;
LDB's attempt to change com-

position of, 50, 51; FDR's concern about, 50-51; Frankfurter and Landis's book about, 124. *See also names of individual cases*
United States v. *Butler*, 36 n 81, 45, 62-63 n 53
Urofsky, Melvin I., 2, 13, 18, 23, 99, 118
utilities, public, 49

Wagner, Robert A., 27, 50
Wagner Act, 121
Wagner-Lewis Bill, 48. *See also* Social Security Act of 1935
Wallace, Henry, 45
War Labor Policies Board, 42
Warren, George, 46
Warren, Samuel D., 5, 68, 127
Wehle, Louis B. (nephew), 24
Weizmann, Chaim, 72, 74, 79, 82
Wheeler, Burton K., 52
Wheeler, Russell R., 31 n 35
White, G. Edward, 144
White, Herbert, 103
Witney v. *California*, 9, 125, 127
Wilson, Woodrow: endorsed for president by LDB, 7; nomination of LDB to U.S. Supreme Court by, 8, 151 n 40;

advised by LDB, 11, 12, 38, 42, 110, 112, 133
Wisconsin Plan for unemployment insurance, 48
Wise, Stephen S., 77, 92, 133
Witt, Nathan, 45
Wooley, Robert W., 11-12
World Zionist Organization, 73, 79
Wyzanski, Charles, 26

Zimmern, Sir Alfred, 95-96 n 17, 141
Zionism, European, 65-66, 72, 94; political versus cultural, 74
—American: LDB as leader in, 7, 8, 9, 11, 25, 29, 65, 67-70, 75, 76, 141-43; proposed reorganization of the movement, 8; Frankfurter's activities on behalf of, 23, 42, 78, 143; LDB's participation in Zionist meeting in 1916, 28-29; definition of 65, 66, 70-72; LDB's financial contributions to, 80-81, 91; and kibbutz movement, 85-95
Zionist Organization of America (ZOA), 80, 84, 90, 94. *See also* Avukah